MW00597528

CATHOLIC CONTROVERSY SERIES

BFSMedia Presents...

MyCatholicSource.com User-Submitted Article:

What's Up With Faustina's Divine Mercy Devotion? *Unanswered Questions & Things You May Not Know*

By M.M. Anthony

+ + +

BFSMedia & MyCatholicSource.com are divisions of B.F.S.

(C) 2013-2017, B.F.S. All Rights Reserved.

First Edition

+ + +

Notice: Use of this material is subject to our Terms of Use

Terms of Use / Disclaimer

This is a MyCatholicSource.com user-submitted article. Note that views of author do not necessarily reflect our views. Content herein is based on an online version of the article. Any visit to our website(s) may require agreement to our terms. For more terms information, visit http://www.mycatholicsource.com/mcs/terms_of_use.htm.

Translations, titles, capitalization, punctuation, wording, references, spelling, etc. of all items herein may vary. Quotations may be partial, out of context, in any order, categorized subjectively, etc. Formatting, explanatory text, links, etc. may have been added to items herein.

We make no guarantee regarding any item herein. All material is provided on an "as is" basis, without warranty of any kind. We are not liable for any loss or damage resulting from reliance on any information contained herein or for any loss or damage due to any error(s) or omission(s). We are not liable for any occurrence whatsoever which may result from any use of this material (including use of any links). All use of the material is at your own risk. By using any material (including links), you agree to hold us harmless for all consequences, damages, etc. - direct or indirect - which may occur in any way connected with any use of this material - regardless of their nature and without limit. By using any material herein, including links, you agree to all our terms. For more terms information, visit http://www.mycatholicsource.com/mcs/terms_of_use.htm.

Note From Author

Before beginning this article, please understand that this is certainly not intended as a treatise against St. Faustina. Based on her diary, St. Faustina apparently does love God much, suffer much, and say many humble things. She claims a deep closeness with God and is apparently absorbed in pleasing Him according to what she sees as His will. This article is also not about whether or not one likes Faustina's message (who wouldn't like a message of mercy?). This is plainly a call to look at the facts concerning this devotion objectively and with an open mind. Admittedly, it won't be popular to pose questions about this well-loved devotion, but what should be feared if one is honestly seeking the truth?

Additional Notes

References herein to "Diary" or "par." (paragraph) refer to applicable portions of Faustina's diary. Various excerpts from Faustina's diary may be included with the text below or may be included at the end of this publication. According to the author, passages provided herein may represent a small sampling of related passages & passages provided may be partial and in no particular order. Author indicates that the article relies on a free online version of Faustina's diary for the text below, along with some minor changes (for example, spelling, capitalization and punctuation changes, merged paragraphs, etc.). For easier reading, we have formatted various items herein and we have provided additional links below.

Please note that the material herein is intended to be presented respectfully, and mindful of 1983 Code of Canon Law Can. 212 §3: "According to the knowledge, competence, and prestige which [the Christian faithful] possess, they have the right and even at times the duty to manifest to the sacred pastors their opinion on matters which pertain to the good of the Church and to make their opinion known to the rest of the Christian faithful, without prejudice to the integrity of faith and morals, with reverence toward their pastors, and attentive to common advantage and the dignity of persons."

Please remember that Church approval of Faustina's diary & her Divine Mercy devotion does NOT guarantee that her alleged experiences are genuine, nor does her canonization. The Church is *unable* to guarantee the authenticity of any apparition outside of Holy Scripture with "absolute certainty."

Furthermore, as St. Thomas Aquinas, Doctor of the Church and "greatest theologian in the history of the Church", reminds: "Faith rests on divine revelations made through the prophets and apostles and set down in the canonical Scriptures, not on revelations, if there by any, made to other holy teachers." And, as St. John of the Cross, Doctor of the Church, warns: "The devil is most pleased when he sees that people desire to accept revelations and are inclined toward them. For then he has an excellent opportunity to inject errors and disparage faith as much as possible."

PART 1

What's Up With Faustina's Divine Mercy Devotion?
Unanswered Questions & Things You May Not Know

By M.M. Anthony

Gaining much popularity in the Catholic Church today is Sister Faustina's (now St. Faustina's) heavily promoted 'Divine Mercy' devotion which is based on mystical experiences she reports in her diary. Although this Polish nun's devotion was first condemned by the Church, it was later 'revived' by (the also Polish) Pope John Paul II. (More on that later.) Despite the great popularity of the devotion, however, few people may know what's really in Faustina's full writings (devotees may typically rely on short summaries), fewer still may have looked at such writings critically. For example, many people have no clue that her 200,000+ word diary contains...

- **contradictions** (see below, #A1), for example...

  - about sisters not being in purgatory

  - about everything being pleasing to God

  - about her not having self-concern

  - different souls who uphold the world

  - about her not being judged

  - that she could thwart God's plans

- doubts

- etc.

- **factual errors / inaccuracies** (see below, #A2), for example...

  - regarding the Ascension

  - receiving viaticum yet not dying

  - difficulties prove a work is God's

  - would not remain in congregation

  - angels/time of mercy

  - reason for Satan being thrown out of heaven

  - etc.

- **exaggerations** (see below, #A3)

- **prophecies that do not materialize** (see below, #A4), for example...

  - about her being in the new congregation

  - about her wearing the habit of the new congregation

  - about her seeing the Feast of mercy implemented

- **scandalous actions** (see below, #A5), for example...

  - forced baptism of adult Jewish woman

  - a seemingly sacrilegious confession

  - Faustina's self-admitted lying / misrepresenting herself

- **theological problems / faulty theology** (see below, #A6), for example...

  - mercy depending on trust rather than sorrow for sins

  - God's 'greatest attribute'

  - supposed 'right' to mercy

  - everyone fulfills His will

  - bad actions not bad based on intention

  - etc.

- **bad / dangerous advice** (see below, #A7), for example...

  - about not calling priest when dying

  - about presumption

  - about following interior inspirations

- **disturbing images** (see below, #A8)

- **an inconceivable attempt to impose new doctrine / promote dangerous practices** (see below, #A9), for example...

  - threatens hell for those who do not adore God's mercy

  - call to trust in mercy as apparent substitute for repentance

  - etc.

- **uncharacteristic behavior & speech attributed to God, the Blessed Virgin Mary, etc.** (see below, #A10), for example...

  - uncharacteristic way they talk

8

- uncharacteristic physical closeness

- transparent clothing / uncovered head

- calling female 'Apostle'

- strange requests

- 'taking her heart'

- tasking her with instructing superiors and priests

- etc.

- **fanciful descriptions that do not seem possible in the literal sense** (see below, #A11)

- **etc.**

...and that she attributes much of this (contradictions, errors, disturbing images, theological problems, etc.) to God himself!

+ + +

Few people may know that Faustina claimed to have seen Jesus...

- **on the ceiling** (see Diary, par. 383)

- **sitting in [!] the chalice**

  "I saw the Infant Jesus who, with hands outstretched toward us, was sitting in the chalice being used at Holy Mass" (Diary, par. 1346)

- **on the curtain**

  "...and on the curtain I saw the very sorrowful Face of Jesus. There were open wounds on His Face, and large tears were falling on my bedspread" (Diary, par. 19)

9

- **sitting at the table waiting for her** (see Diary, par. 1782)

- **running on the altar**

  "A moment later, the Infant Jesus ran with joy to the center of the altar" (Diary, par. 677)

- **playfully on the altar** (see Diary, par. 312)

- **on the altar turning the pages of her diary**

  "I saw the Lord Jesus on the altar, in a white garment, His hand holding the notebook in which I write these things. Throughout the entire meditation Jesus kept turning the pages of the notebook" (Diary, par. 459)

- **with her (not the priest!) in the confessional** (see Diary, par. 654)

- **at her side** (see Diary, par. 9, 40, 960)

- **next to her kneeler** (see Diary, par. 526)

- **resting in her hands**

  "I saw the little Jesus, who came out from the Host and rested in my hands." (Diary, par. 406)

- **holding on to her kneeler (as an infant!)**

  "...the Infant Jesus standing by my kneeler and holding on to it with His two little hands." (Diary, par. 566)

- **leaning over her**

  "I saw the Lord Jesus leaning over me, and He asked, My daughter, what are you writing?" (Diary, par. 1693)

- **speaking to her from the tabernacle**

  "I brought my head close to the tabernacle, knocked [!] and said, 'Jesus, look at the great difficulties I am having because of the painting of this image.' And I heard a voice from the tabernacle, My daughter, your sufferings will not last much longer." (Diary, par. 152)

- **in a brightness "greater than the light of the sun"**

  "I saw Jesus in a brightness greater than the light of the sun." (Diary, par. 1669)

- **in her soul**

  "Often during Mass, I see the Lord in my soul" (Diary, par. 411)

- **in the sky**

  "I saw the Sacred Heart of Jesus in the sky" (Diary, par. 1796)

- **with "Precious pearls and diamonds...pouring forth from the wound in His Heart"**

  "Today I saw the Crucified Lord Jesus. Precious pearls and diamonds were pouring forth from the wound in His Heart." (Diary, par. 1687)

- **etc.**

+ + +

She claims she sees or hears Jesus all the time - but no one else who is there sees or hears Him. Furthermore, all of heaven seems immediately on call to answer Faustina's questions and assist her whenever she needs anything - no matter how

mundane. And some are also uncharacteristically close with her physically (e.g. Jesus snuggling, Mary holding her close to herself). She alleges visions, voices or special encounters with...

- **God the Father** (e.g. see Diary, par. 60, 626)

- **The Holy Trinity** (e.g. see Diary, par. 27, 451, 474, 1670)

- **Jesus (as infant, as crucified, in a great brightness, etc.)** (see Diary, par. 648, 659, 675, etc., etc.)

- **Blessed Virgin Mary** (see Diary, par. 11, 25, 33, 182, etc., etc.)

- **St. Joseph** (see Diary, par. 608, 846, 1203, 1442)

- **Disciples** (referring to those alive when Jesus walked the earth) (see Diary, par. 642)

- **Guardian Angel** (see Diary, par. 20, 314, 419, etc.)

- **Satan / devils** (even "a great multitude of demons") (see Diary, par. 173, 411, 418, 520, 741, etc.)

- **St. Peter** (see Diary, par. 1044)

- **The Pope** (see Diary, par. 368, 1044, 1080)

- **St. Michael** (see Diary, par. 706)

- **St. Barbara** (see Diary, par. 1251)

- **St. Ignatius** (see Diary, par. 448)

- **Souls in purgatory** (see Diary, par. 20, 58, etc.)

- **a 'multitude of malicious figures'** (see Diary, par. 416)

- **one of the seven spirits that stand before the throne of God** (see Diary, par. 471)

- **an angel, the executor of divine wrath** (see Diary, par. 474)

- **the throne of the Lamb of God and before the throne three Saints: Stanislaus Kostka, Andrew Bobola and Prince Casimir, who were interceding for Poland** (see Diary, par. 689)

- **pictures that come to life** (see Diary, par. 529, 851)

- **a crucifix on her breast that comes to life**

  "I went for five- minute adoration, when suddenly I saw the crucifix I have on my breast come alive. Jesus said to me..." (Diary, par. 669)

- **another crucifix that comes to life**

  "Then I looked at the crucifix and saw that Jesus. head was turned towards the refectory, and His lips were moving" (Diary, par. 352)

- **Cenacle** (see Diary, par. 684)

- **Apostles** (see Diary, par. 757, 1710)

- **heaven** (see Diary, par. 777)

- **angels** (see Diary, par. 394, 630)

- **angels singing in various tones** (see Diary, par. 1111)

- **spirits**

"Then I saw one of the seven spirits near me, radiant as at other times, under a form of light. I constantly saw him beside me when I was riding on the train. I saw an angel standing on every church we passed, but surrounded by a light which was paler than that of the spirit who was accompanying me on the journey, and each of these spirits who were guarding the churches bowed his head to the spirit who was near me." (Diary, par. 630)

- **saints** (see Diary, par. 683, 1604)

- **a Seraph who gave her Holy Communion more than a dozen times** (see Diary, par. 1676)

- **a Cherub to guard the gate**

"I saw a little white cloud and, in it, a Cherub with his hands joined" (Diary, par. 1271)

- **an angel who sings out her whole life history**

"Then I heard an angel who sang out my whole life history and everything it comprised. I was surprised, but also strengthened." (Diary, par. 1202) *[Note: She does not indicate that the angel's singing out her whole life history took very long]*

- **the stable of Bethlehem filled with great radiance where the blessed Virgin Mary was wrapping Jesus in swaddling clothes while Saint Joseph slept** (see Diary, par. 1442)

- **hell** (see Diary, par. 741)

- **purgatory** (see Diary, par. 412)

- **dead/dying people** (see Diary, par. 314, 515, etc.)

- **a huge crowd of disciples** (see Diary, par. 1710)

- **an "infinite [!] multitude of souls" who were praising His goodness** (see Diary, par. 1681)

- **the Sacred Heart of Jesus in the sky** (see Diary, par. 1796)

- **birds**

    "...the birds were singing and chirping their adoration of God and said to me, 'Rejoice and be happy, Sister Faustina'" (Diary, par. 1120)

    "The next day, during Holy Mass, I saw three white doves soaring from the altar toward heaven" (Diary, par. 748) *[Note: The doves here are apparently symbolic of human souls, unlike in the New Testament where the Holy Spirit is represented as a dove]*

+ + +

She supposedly...

- **has visions** (numerous times in Diary)

- **hears voices** (numerous times in Diary)

- **talks with Jesus** (numerous times in Diary)

- **touches Jesus** (numerous times in Diary)

- **receives special knowledge / 'divine illuminations'** (numerous times in Diary)

- **embraces dead people** (see Diary, par. 594)

- **holds Jesus' hand**

"and Jesus gave me His hand, sat me at His side"
(Diary, par. 1563)

- **is "clasped" by Jesus to His Heart** (see Diary, par. 928)

- **sits next to Jesus / sits by Jesus' side** (for example, see Diary, par. 431)

- **throws herself into Jesus' arms** (see Diary, par. 1824)

- **holds the infant Jesus who talks to her**

"Today during Holy Mass, I saw the Infant Jesus near my kneeler. He appeared to be about one year old, and He asked me to take Him in my arms. When I did take Him in my arms, He cuddled up close to my bosom and said, It is good for Me to be close to your heart." (Diary, par. 1481)

- **reproaches a saint** (see Diary, par. 448)

- **is drawn into the bosom of the Most Holy Trinity** (see Diary, par. 1670)

- **is left alone with the infant Jesus in Bethlehem**

"I saw the stable of Bethlehem filled with great radiance. The Blessed Virgin, all lost in the deepest of love, was wrapping Jesus in swaddling clothes, but Saint Joseph was still asleep. Only after the Mother of God put Jesus in the manger, did the light of God awaken Joseph, who was also praying. But after a while, I was left alone with the Infant Jesus who stretched out His little hands to me, and I understood that I was to take Him in my arms. Jesus pressed His head against my heart and gave me to know, by His profound gaze, how good He found it to be next to my heart." (Diary, par. 1442)

- **is left alone with the infant Jesus after Mary and St. Joseph hand Him off to her and suddenly disappear**

"Just then, I saw Our Lady with the Infant Jesus, and the Holy Old Man [St. Joseph] standing behind them. The most holy Mother said to me, Take My Dearest Treasure, and She handed me the Infant Jesus. When I took the Infant Jesus in my arms, the Mother of God and Saint Joseph disappeared. I was left alone with the Infant Jesus." (Diary, par. 608)

- **experiences & lives through the whole Passion of Jesus instantly in her heart** (see Diary, par. 1663)

- **takes 'her place'[!] on the altar** (see Diary, par. 31)

- **receives instant answers / assistance** (numerous times in diary)

- **receives special instruction and embraces from Jesus & Mary** (numerous times in diary)

+ + +

Sometimes in apparent contrast to the known Jesus (who is the same "yesterday, today, and forever", Heb. 13:8), Faustina's version of Jesus is... *[Note: for sample passages relating to these items, see below, #B]*

- **doting / attentive / "captivated"**

- **rather weak / a pushover, who bends to her desires and whose hands can be "tied"**

- **preferential / picks favorites**

- **sensitive**

17

- constantly reassuring / consoling / comforting / cheering her on

- sad

- complaining

- still suffering

- desperate sounding

- in need of help

- ostensibly lacking some knowledge (he asks questions, he is 'looking for souls' to lavish graces on)

- capable of being "surprised" and "very surprised"

- reluctant to exercise justice

- talkative during Mass (even as an infant)

- repetitive

- an 'Indian giver'

- and one who gives instant feedback

- tries to delay suffering

- 'demands' a lot *[Note: Her diary speaks of God 'demanding' various things from her, yet I do not see in Scripture where Jesus ever told anyone personally that he 'demanded' something in particular from them]*

- discloses new doctrine

- speaks uncharacteristically

- lavishes praise on Faustina

- tasks her with instructing priests & superiors

- and is someone who would make odd requests, impersonate a priest, and who would seem to prefer Faustina's company rather than being in heaven

- and who blesses her pen, moves a cloud to increase her comfort, instructs her in interpersonal communication, advises her regarding eating, arranges a retreat for her, has a private room prepared for her, helps her with her chores, offers her a new world to live in, promises her a permanent income...

+++

Faustina herself seems... *[Note: For sample passages relating to these items, see below, #C]*

- overly dramatic

- pretty sensitive

- emotional

- insensitive to other's concerns with respect to herself (she seems unable to see things from their perspective)

- rather easily annoyed

- somewhat self-centered (e.g. about how people treat her, about what she suffers for others, about how people don't trust her alleged visions)

- up and down a lot ('an emotional roller coaster')

- to need a lot of reassurance

- sometimes lacking in fear of the Lord

- to lack normal reactions to having a life filled with alleged supernatural events/promises (humdrum, day to day - yet she claims to be united with God like no other person before and to have a special closeness, a more intimate relationship with Jesus than all others)

- naïve / credulous / not discerning

- narcissistic (self-important in her alleged mission, talks about the good she does, reproaches a saint)

- seems to live in another world where visions are constant/common and normal (even if their content is disturbing and uncharacteristic of the alleged participants - where the Almighty God and the Mother of God & others are always at her beck and call for whatever her need may be) and those who question the alleged appearances just don't understand the graces she's received or they're in league with the devil

- sometimes weepy, yet more powerful than heavenly beings - she was even able to make an angel, the executor of divine wrath 'helpless', and she was able to calm storms, etc.

- sometimes out of touch with reality / strange sense of reality

- to have visions of grandeur

- to mention her sufferings and mistreatment a lot

+ + +

Yet she claims many special graces and a special closeness with & praise from God and others. For example...

- **She claims that Jesus is uniting Himself with her "so intimately as with no other creature"**

  "I suddenly saw the Lord Jesus, who spoke these words to me...That is why I am uniting Myself with you so intimately as with no other creature." (Diary, par. 707)

- **She claims that she won't undergo judgment**

  "I heard this voice in my soul: From today on, do not fear God's judgment, for you will not be judged." (Diary, par. 374)

- **She claims that the Blessed Virgin Mary has a "special and exclusive" relationship with her by God's command**

  "Before Holy Communion I saw the Blessed Mother inconceivably beautiful. Smiling at me She said to me, My daughter, at God's command I am to be, in a special and exclusive way your Mother" (Diary, par. 1414)

- **She claims that St. Michael the Archangel is to take "special care" of her by order of God**

  "On the Feast of Saint Michael the Archangel, I saw by my side that great Leader, who spoke these words to me: 'The Lord has ordered me to take special care of you.'" (Diary, par. 706)

- **She claims St. Joseph gives her "special help and protection"**

21

"Saint Joseph urged me to have a constant devotion to him. He himself told me to recite three prayers [the Our Father, Hail Mary, and Glory be] and the Memorare once every day. He looked at me with great kindness and gave me to know how much he is supporting this work [of mercy]. He has promised me this special help and protection. I recite the requested prayers every day and feel his special protection." (Diary, par. 1203)

- **She claims she has "first place" among the virgins (there is not even a mention here of the Blessed Virgin Mary!)**

"I see your love, so pure and true that I give you first place among the virgins." (Diary, par. 282)

- **She claims that "one of the seven spirits who stand before the throne of God day and night and give Him ceaseless praise" accompanies her everywhere**

"This spirit does not leave me for a single moment, but accompanies me everywhere." (Diary, par. 471)

- **She claims to have seen "the grandeur and the inconceivable holiness of God"**

"Suddenly, my spirit was united with God, and in that instant I saw the grandeur and the inconceivable holiness of God" (Diary, par. 471)

- **She claims to "know the entire essence [!] of God"**

"in one moment, I come to know the entire essence of God." (Diary, par. 770)

- **She claims she felt "totally immersed" in God and "penetrated by" God** "once again the majesty of God overwhelmed me. I felt that I was immersed in God, totally immersed in Him and penetrated by Him" (Diary, par. 491)

- **She claims Jesus allowed her to "penetrate His interior"**

"Jesus allowed me to penetrate His interior" (Diary, par. 757)

- **She claims Jesus had her "very much" on His mind 2,000 years ago when he instituted the Holy Eucharist on Holy Thursday**

"During the June devotions, the Lord said to me, My daughter, My favor rests in your heart. When on Holy Thursday I left Myself in the Blessed Sacrament, you were very much on My mind." (Diary, par. 1774)

- **She claims Jesus called her a "sweet grape" and that he wants "others to have a share in the juice that is flowing within (her)"**

"During one conference, Jesus said to me, You are a sweet grape in a chosen cluster; I want others to have a share in the juice that is flowing within you." (Diary, par. 393)

- **She claims Jesus offered to instantly create "a new world" for her to live in**

"Once, I suddenly saw Jesus in great majesty, and He spoke these words to me: My daughter, if you wish, I will this instant create a new world, more beautiful than this one, and you will live there for the rest of your life." (Diary, par. 587)

- **She claims Jesus took off his golden girdle and tied it around her waist**

"Jesus appeared suddenly at my side clad in a white garment with a golden girdle around His waist, and He said to me, I give you eternal love that your purity may be untarnished and as a sign that you will never be subject to temptations against purity. Jesus took off His golden cincture and tied it around my waist." (Diary, par. 40)

- **She claims Jesus took her heart**

"On my way back, as I was passing close to the little chapel, I saw Jesus standing in the doorway. He said to me, Go ahead, but I am taking your heart. Suddenly I felt that I had no heart in my chest." (Diary, par. 42)

- **She claims she has saved "so many" souls from damnation and that Satan therefore burns with a "particular hatred" for her**

"I heard a voice in my soul, You are united to Me; fear nothing. But know, my child, that Satan hates you; he hates every soul, but he burns with a particular hatred for you, because you have snatched so many souls from his dominion." (Diary, par. 412)

- **She claims to have relived the Mother of God's interior sentiments**

"I relived her interior sentiments." (Diary, par. 182)

- **She claims to have been enveloped by "God's presence", "His majesty", "God's omnipotence", "His Trinitarian Being", etc.**

(See Diary, par. 252, 259, 409, 574, 629, 635, 644, 715, 1056, etc.)

- She claims she was "instantly snatched up before the Throne of God"

"I was instantly snatched up before the Throne of God." (Diary, par. 474)

- She claims to have "intimate knowledge" of the Lord and a "mutual understanding" with Jesus that no one can comprehend

"I would not want to change places even with a Seraph, as regards the interior knowledge of God which He Himself has given me. The intimate knowledge I have of the Lord is such as no creature can comprehend, particularly, the depth of his mercy that envelops me." (Diary, par. 1049)

"Our hearts have a mutual understanding, and no one of humankind will comprehend this." (Diary, par. 478)

- She claims special communication with the dying (for example, see Diary, par. 835)

- She claims to have known "more distinctly, than ever before, the Three divine Persons, the Father, the Son, and the Holy Spirit" (see Diary, par. 472)

- She claims that she was a consolation to Jesus in the Garden of Olives

"My daughter, know that your ardent love and the compassion you have for Me were a consolation to Me in the Garden [of Olives]." (Diary, par. 1664)

- She claims an "uninterrupted communion with Jesus" for an entire retreat

"Throughout the whole retreat, I was in uninterrupted communion with Jesus and entered into an intimate relationship with Him with all the might of my heart." (Diary, par. 467)

- **She claims that her soul was filled with a surge of light**

"a surge of light filled my soul" (Diary, par. 1617)

- **She claims God's presence penetrated her "completely in a way that could be sensed", and that her "spirit was flooded with light" and that her "body participated in this as well"**

"His presence penetrated me completely in a way that could be sensed. My spirit was flooded with light, and my body participated in this as well." (Diary, par. 627)

- **She claims she feels the "constant presence of God" "without any effort"**

"I feel the constant presence of God without any effort of my soul." (Diary, par. 411)

- **She claims Jesus' presence accompanies her "everywhere"**

"I go everywhere with Jesus; His presence accompanies me everywhere." (Diary, par. 486)

- **She claims she experienced "the whole ocean and abyss of [God's] fathomless mercy"**

"the Lord gave me to experience the whole ocean and abyss of His fathomless mercy." (Diary, par. 1073)

- **She claims she's seen the Lord "in all His majesty"**

"I saw the Lord Jesus in all His majesty" (Diary, par. 1246)

- **She claims the Blessed Virgin Mary instructed her about the will of God and how to apply it**

"...the Most Holy Mother who instructed me about the will of God and how to apply it to my life" (Diary, par. 1244)

- **She claims to have been united "in a particular way" with God and the Blessed Virgin Mary**

"During Holy Mass today, I was united in a particular way with God and His Immaculate Mother." (Diary, par. 843)

- **She says she distinctly feels a "power" defending and protecting her from the blows of the enemy**

"I feel that there is a power which is defending me and protecting me from the blows of the enemy. It guards and defends me. I feel it very distinctly; it is as if I am being shielded by the shadow of his wings." (Diary, par. 1799)

- **She claims to be "intimately" united with Jesus, and that their hearts "understand each other"**

"O my Lord and Creator, You alone, beyond all these gifts, give Your own Self to me and unite Yourself intimately with Your miserable creature. Here, without searching for words, our hearts understand each other." (Diary, par. 1692)

- **She claims Jesus unites Himself with her closer than with anyone else**

"Then I heard these words: With no other soul do I unite Myself as closely and in such a way as I do with you" (Diary, par. 587)

- **She claims Jesus is "wounded" more by a mere "glance" of hers directed at someone other than Himself than He is by "many sins[!]" committed by someone else**

"On one occasion, I heard these words within me: Every movement of your heart is known to Me. Know, My daughter, that once glance of yours directed at someone else would wound Me more than many sins committed by another person." (Diary, par. 588)

- **She claims a more intimate relationship with Jesus than the angels have**

"I heard these words in my soul: You are My spouse forever; your chastity should be greater than that of the angels, for I call no angel to such intimacy as I do you." (Diary, par. 534)

- **She claims "the whole mystery" depended on her that God "waited" for her consent**

"the Lord gave me to know that the whole mystery depended on me... I felt that God was waiting for my word, for my consent." (Diary, par. 136)

- **She claims God's presence "pervaded" her soul, that she was "plunged into the ocean of His divinity" and that "all that exists" is hers**

"When I approached the altar, God's presence pervaded my soul, I was plunged into the ocean of His divinity, and Jesus said to me, My daughter, all that exists is yours." (Diary, par. 969)

- **She claims to "often" receive "light and the knowledge of the interior life of God and of God's intimate disposition"**

  "I often receive light and the knowledge of the interior life of God and of God's intimate disposition" (Diary, par. 1102)

- **She claims to receive "sudden lights" which allow her to know things as God does**

  "These are sudden lights which permit me to know things as God sees them, regarding matters of both the interior and the exterior world." (Diary, par. 733)

- **She claims the Blessed Virgin Mary is "always" with her**

  "She alone is always with me. She, like a good Mother, watches over all my trials and efforts." (Diary, par. 798)

- **She claims long periods of being united with God**

  "I felt that I am closely united to the Godhead. His omnipotence enveloped my whole being. Throughout the whole day I felt the closeness of God in a special manner; and although my duties prevented me throughout the whole day from going to chapel even for a moment, there was not a moment when I was not united with God. I felt Him within me more distinctly than ever." (Diary, par. 346)

- **She claims Jesus brought her into "close intimacy" with Him, and that all that concerns His Being was imparted into her**

  "And He brought me into such close intimacy with Himself that my heart was espoused to His Heart in a loving union, and I could feel the faintest stir of His Heart and he, of mine. The fire of my created love was

joined to the ardor of His eternal love. This one grace
surpasses all others in its immensity. His Trinitarian
Being enveloped me entirely, and I am totally immersed
in Him. My littleness is, as it were, wrestling with this
Immortal Might One. I am immersed in
incomprehensible love and incomprehensible torture
because of His Passion. All that concerns His Being is
imparted to me also." (Diary, par. 1056)

- **She claims Jesus told her she was doing God's will
  perfectly and that He was uniting Himself with her in a
  "special and intimate way"**

"And Jesus told me that I was doing the will of God
perfectly ...and for this reason I am uniting Myself with
you and communing with you in a special and intimate
way." (Diary, par. 603)

- **She feels she is the object of God's "special action" and
  there is a special mystery that distinguishes her from
  "every other soul"**

"I feel that I am the object of His special action. For His
inscrutable purposes and unfathomable decrees, He
united me to Himself in a special way and allows me to
penetrate His incomprehensible mysteries. There is one
mystery which unites me with the Lord, of which no one
– not even angels – may know. And even if I wanted to
tell of it, I would not know how to express it. And yet, I
live by it and will live by it for ever. This mystery
distinguishes me from every other soul here on earth or
in eternity." (Diary, par. 824)

- **She says Jesus obtained a special grace for her when He
  was before Herod 2,000 years ago**

"My daughter, when I was before Herod, I obtained a
grace for you" (Diary, par. 1164)

- **She says the Lord's gaze rests upon her "before any other creature"**

"My dearest child, your every stirring is reflected in My Heart. My gaze rests kindly upon you before any other creature." (Diary, par. 1700)

- **She says the Lord is "jealous" of her heart**

"At that moment, the Lord gave me to know how jealous He is of my heart." (Diary, par. 1542)

- **She claims the Lord promised her a "permanent income"**

"Suddenly I head these words in my soul: My daughter, I assure you of a permanent income on which you will live." (Diary, par. 548)

- **She claims Jesus is concerned about "every beat" of her heart and "thirsts" for her love**

"I am concerned about every beat of your heart. Every stirring of your love is reflected in My Heart. I thirst for your love." (Diary, par. 1542)

- **She feels Jesus was so very anxious to be received by her in Holy Communion that He would have leaped out of a priest's hands to come to her if the priest had "tarried a little longer"**

"After that night of suffering, when the priest entered my cell with the Lord Jesus, such fervor filled my whole being that I felt that if the priest had tarried a little longer, Jesus himself would have leaped out of his hand and come to me. After Holy Communion the Lord said to me, If the priest had not brought Me to you, I would have come Myself under the same species." (Diary, par. 1458-1459)

- **She claims the infant Jesus left his Mother's arms[!] and approached her**

"I saw the Mother of God with the Infant Jesus in Her arms, and I also saw my confessor kneeling at Her feet and talking with her. I did not understand what he was saying to Her, because I was busy talking with the Infant Jesus, who came down from His Mother's arms and approached me." (Diary, par. 330)

- **She feels she is being lifted up into the "inner life of God"**

"This Mighty Ruler of heaven has taken entire possession of my soul. I feel that I am being lifted up above earth and heaven into the inner life of God" (Diary, par. 734)

- **She says she has been allowed to understand God's interior life**

"On one occasion, God's presence pervaded my whole being, and my mind was mysteriously enlightened in respect to His Essence. He allowed me to understand His interior life." (Diary, par. 911)

- **She claims to have felt the presence of the Holy Trinity in her soul**

"Once after Holy Communion, I heard these words: You are Our dwelling place. At that moment, I felt in my soul the presence of the Holy Trinity, the Father, the Son, and the Holy Spirit." (Diary, par. 451)

- **She says she feels completely transformed into Him**

"At the first altar, a flame issued from the Host and pierced my heart, and I heard a voice, Here is My resting place. Ardor burst into flame in my heart. I felt that I am transformed completely into Him." (Diary, par. 1140)

- **She claims Jesus teaches her and that their hearts are "fused as one"**

"Jesus often visits me in this seclusion, teaches me, reassures me, rebukes me, and admonished me. He Himself forms my heart according to His divine wishes and likings, but always with much goodness and mercy. Our hearts are fused as one." (Diary, par. 1024)

- **She claims that Jesus says their intimacy is an exclusive one**

"know that yours is an exclusive intimacy with Me" (Diary, par. 1693)

- **She claims to feel God's presence physically**

"God's presence pervades my soul, not only in a spiritual way, but I feel it in a physical way also." (Diary, par. 747)

- **She claims many other extraordinary things...**

"An extraordinary, divine power came over me after that confession" (Diary, par. 257)

"an extraordinary fire was enkindled in my soul" (Diary, par. 439)

"my soul felt extraordinary strength" (Diary, par. 527)

"I feel an extraordinary force driving me to action" (Diary, par. 615)

"an extraordinary light filled my soul" (Diary, par. 623)

"God's presence filled me in an extraordinary way" (Diary, par. 675)

"The extraordinary light that allowed me to see His majesty" (Diary, par. 757)

"this extraordinary grace of union which has continued to this day" (Diary, par. 770)

"These extraordinary flashes from the Lord educate my soul" (Diary, par. 852)

"the Lord grants me an extraordinary spirit of prayer" (Diary, par. 971)

"an extraordinary understanding of many things was communicated to my intellect" (Diary, par. 1048)

"an extraordinary peace and power filled my soul" (Diary, par. 1150)

"an extraordinary light remained in my soul" (Diary, par. 1153)

"I experience an extraordinary equilibrium" (Diary, par. 1334)

"I felt an extraordinary strength in my soul" (Diary, par. 1704)

+ + +

However, Jesus tells us in Holy Scripture that there is no one born of woman greater than St. John the Baptist (not even St. Faustina!) and yet the least in the kingdom of heaven is greater than St. John the Baptist...

- Mt. 11:11: "Amen, I say to you, among those born of women there has been none greater than John the Baptist; yet the least in the kingdom of heaven is greater than he."

- Lk. 7:28: " I tell you, among those born of women, no one is greater than John; yet the least in the kingdom of God is greater than he."

Even though Jesus explicitly tells us in Holy Scripture that St. John the Baptist is the greatest on earth of those born of woman, Jesus...

- never united himself more closely with St. John the Baptist than with any other creature

- never gave St. John the Baptist "first place" among the virgins

- never says he had St. John the Baptist on the mind when he instituted the Holy Eucharist

- never called St. John the Baptist a "sweet grape"

- never offered to create a "new world" for St. John the Baptist to live in

- never said he united himself with St. John the Baptist more closely than with anyone else

- never said that there is something that distinguishes St. John the Baptist "from every other souls here on earth or in eternity"

- never said his gaze rested on St. John the Baptist before any other creature

- never offered St. John the Baptist a permanent income

- never said he was concerned about "every beat" of St. John the Baptist's heart

- never says he and St. John the Baptist have an "exclusive intimacy"

Nor was Jesus known to say or do some of these things even for the greatest saint ever - His own blessed Mother! Yet he supposedly said and did all these things for St. Faustina?

+ + +

In Faustina's writings, we also find a claim that the Blessed Virgin Mary "gave [Faustina] to understand that [she] had faithfully fulfilled the will of God and had thus found favor in His eyes" (Diary, par. 449). Compare this to Holy Scripture where we read...

> Lk. 1:30: Then the angel said to her, "Do not be afraid, Mary, for you have found favor with God."

This passage from St. Luke is the only passage I can find in the entire New Testament where an individual - namely, the Blessed Virgin Mary - is singled out as "finding favor" with God. Yet Faustina applies this sentient to herself by means of the Blessed Virgin Mary. This is not the only passage in Faustina's diary where items from Scripture seem turned around and applied to Faustina. Her diary also contains these items...

> **Well-beloved daughter**: "I heard the words, You are My well-beloved daughter" (Diary, par. 1681)
> *[Compare with Mk. 1:11: And a voice came from the heavens, "You are my beloved Son; with you I am well pleased."]*

> **Did not recognize time of visitation**: "When once I asked the Lord Jesus how He could tolerate so many sins and crimes and not punish them, the Lord answered

36

me, I have eternity for punishing [these], and so I am prolonging the time of mercy for the sake of [sinners]. But woe to them if they do not recognize this time of My visitation[!]." (Diary, par. 1160) *[Compare with Lk. 19:44: "They will smash you to the ground and your children within you, and they will not leave one stone upon another within you because you did not recognize the time of your visitation."]*

Mystery depending on her: "When the vision ended, a cold sweat bathed my forehead. Jesus made it known to me that, even if I did not give my consent to this, I could still be saved; and He would not lessen His graces, but would still continue to have the same intimate relationship with me, so that even if I did not consent to make this sacrifice, God's generosity would not lessen thereby. And the Lord gave me to know that the whole mystery depended on me, on my free consent to the sacrifice given with full use of my faculties... I felt that God was waiting for my word, for my consent. Then my spirit immersed itself in the Lord, and I said, 'Do with me as You please. I subject myself to Your will. As of today, Your holy will shall be my nourishment, and I will be faithful to Your commands with the help of Your grace. Do with me as You please. I beg You, O Lord, be with me at every moment of my life.'" (Diary, par. 135-136) *[Compare with Lk. 1:38: Mary said, "Behold, I am the handmaid of the Lord. May it be done to me according to your word."]*

As if Faustina could determine the time of her own death: "O my Jesus, I now embrace the whole world and ask You for mercy for it. When You tell me, O God, that it is enough, that Your holy will has been completely accomplished, then, my Savior, in union with You, I will commit my soul into the hands of the Heavenly Father, full of trust in Your unfathomable mercy. And when I stand at the foot of Your throne, the first hymn that I will sing will be one to Your mercy."

(Diary, par. 1582) *[Compare with Lk. 23:46: Jesus cried out in a loud voice, "Father, into your hands I commend my spirit"; and when he had said this he breathed his last.]*

+ + +

Also, Faustina claims to be the object of God's special praise & pleasure [e.g. "the Most High Lord is pleased in me and tells me so Himself" (Diary, par. 947), and "God gives me to know interiorly that every beat of my heart is pleasing to Him, and when He shows me that He loves me in a special way." (Diary, par. 1121)]. The Lord supposedly also said the following to Sister Faustina...

- "My daughter, My pleasure and delight, nothing will stop me from granting you graces." (Diary, par. 1182)

- "I am pleased with what you are doing." (Diary, par. 1499)

- "Let it be confirmed and engraved on your heart that I am always with you" (Diary, par. 1499)

- "My daughter, those words of your heart are pleasing to Me" (Diary, par. 929)

- "My child you are My delight, you are the comfort of My Heart. I grant you as many graces as you can hold." (Diary, par. 164)

- "Beloved pearl of My Heart, I see your love so pure, purer than that of the angels [!], and all the more so because you keep fighting. For your sake I bless the world. I see your efforts to please Me, and they delight My Heart." (Diary, par. 1061)

- "I am delighted with your love. Your sincere love is as pleasing to My Heart as the fragrance of a rosebud at

38

morningtide, before the sun has taken the dew from it. The freshness of your heart captivates Me; that is why I united Myself with you more closely than with any other creature[!]" (Diary, par. 1546)

- "Suddenly, I saw the Lord Jesus near me, and He graciously said to me, All this I created for you, My spouse; and know that all this beauty is nothing compared to what I have prepared for you in eternity." (Diary, par. 158)

- "Suddenly, I heard these words: You are My delightful dwelling place; My Spirit rests in you." (Diary, par. 346)

- "I heard these words within me: You are My joy; you are My heart's delight." (Diary, par. 27)

- "And the Lord said to me, You are the delight of My Heart; from today on, every one of your acts, even the very smallest, will be a delight to My eyes, whatever you do. At that moment I felt transconsecrated. My earthly body was the same, but my soul was different; God was now living in it with the totality of His delight." (Diary, par. 137)

- "You are the honor and glory of My Passion." (Diary, par. 282)

- "He said to me, You are My Heart" (Diary, par. 1666)

- "My daughter, delight of My heart, it is with pleasure that I look into your soul. I bestow many graces only because of you. I also withhold My punishments only because of you." (Diary, par. 1193)

- "I saw Jesus, and He said to me, You are My great joy; your love and your humility make Me leave the heavenly throne and unite Myself with you." (Diary, par. 512)

- "Jesus said to me, My host, you are refreshment for My tormented Heart." (Diary, par. 1056)

- "Today, I heard these words in my soul: Host pleasing to My Father, know, My daughter, that the entire Holy Trinity finds Its special delight in you" (Diary, par. 955)

- "My daughter, your heart is My repose; it is My delight." (Diary, par. 339)

- "My daughter, your heart is My heaven." (Diary, par. 238)

- "You are my dwelling place and my constant repose. For your sake I will withhold the hand which punishes; for your sake I bless the earth." (Diary, par. 431)

- "My Heart is pleased with you, and for your sake I am blessing the earth." (Diary, par. 980)

- "And your heart is My constant dwelling place" (Diary, par. 723)

- "Your heart is My repose." (Diary, par. 268)

- "You are solace in My dying hour." (Diary, par. 310)

- "You have great and incomprehensible rights over My Heart" (Diary, par. 718)

- "My ears and heart are inclined towards you, and your words are dear to Me." (Diary, par. 921)

- "My daughter, My delight is to unite myself with you." (Diary, par. 954)

- "He looked at me and said, Beloved daughter of My Heart, you are My solace amidst terrible torments." (Diary, par. 1058)

And the Blessed Virgin Mary supposedly confirmed...

"You [Faustina] are a dwelling place pleasing to the living God; in you He dwells continuously with love and delight." (Diary, par. 785)

+ + +

What saint has ever had so much praise lavished upon them by God? What saint has ever been singled out for so many special encounters & so many special favors? Yet scripture tells us clearly that God shows no partiality...

- Wisdom 6:7: "For the Lord of all shows no partiality"

- Acts 10:34: "Then Peter proceeded to speak and said, 'In truth, I see that God shows no partiality.'"

- Rom. 2:11: "There is no partiality with God."

- Eph. 6:9: "Masters, act in the same way toward them, and stop bullying, knowing that both they and you have a Master in heaven and that with him there is no partiality."

+ + +

Also - and I think this is rather strange for a saint - Faustina frequently refers to her own holiness / sanctity / perfection / goodness ...

- "Welcome to you, New Year, in the course of which my perfection will be accomplished." (Diary, par. 1449)

- "...on one occasion a certain person suffered because of my sanctity" (Diary, par. 1571)

- "...the Lord was looking with love on my virtues and my heroic efforts" (Diary, par. 758)

- "In the clear rays of your love, my soul has lost its tartness and has become a sweet and ripe fruit." (Diary, par. 1363)

- "I know what His divine Heart desires, and I always do what will please Him the most." (Diary, par. 411)

- "Jesus, You Yourself have deigned to lay the foundations of my sanctity" (Diary, par. 1331)

- "I have come to a knowledge of my destiny; that is, an inward certainty that I will attain sanctity." (Diary, par. 1362)

- "I have always, always, fulfilled His will, as he has made it known to me." (Diary, par. 1667)

- "Now I can be wholly useful to the Church by my personal sanctity" (Diary, par. 1364)

- "they often take advantage of my goodness" (Diary, par. 1446)

- "My lips shall fall silent in great humility." (Diary, par. 1653)

- "...my heart became so wonderfully attracted to these virtues (humility, purity, love of God); and I practice them faithfully." (Diary, par. 1415) *[Doesn't it kind of contradict humility when a person says they practice the virtue of humility faithfully?]*

- "When Jesus ravished me by His beauty and drew me to Himself, I then saw what in my soul was displeasing to Him and made up my mind to remove it, cost what it may; and aided by the grace of God I did remove it at once. This magnanimity pleased the Lord" (Diary, par. 293)

- "But I, too, have found a way to give perfect glory to the incomprehensible mercy of God." (Diary, par. 835)

+ + +

And - also kind of strange for a saint - she often complains about / criticizes others and talks about the treatment she receives...

- "Community life is difficult in itself, but it is doubly difficult to get along with proud souls." (Diary, par. 1522)

- "A priest who is not at peace with himself will not be able to inspire peace in another soul." (Diary, par. 75)

- "Once during recreation, one of the sister directresses said that the lay sisters were without feelings, and so could be treated stiffly. I was sorry to see that the sister directresses know so little about the lay sisters and judge them only from appearances." (Diary, par. 1716)

- "Once, when I was in the kitchen with Sister N., she got a little upset with me and, as a punishment, ordered me to sit on the table while she herself continued to work hard, cleaning and scrubbing. And while I was sitting there, the sisters came along and were astounded to find me sitting on the table, and each one had her say. One said that I was a loafer and another, 'What an eccentric!' I was a postulant at the time. Others said, 'What kind of a sister will she make?' Still, I could not get down because sister had ordered me to sit there by virtue of obedience until she told me to get down. Truly, God alone knows how many acts of self-denial it took." (Diary, par. 151)

- "I had many opportunities to practice virtue. I listened to people pour out their grievances, and I saw that no heart was joyful, because no heart truly loved God; and this did not surprise me at all." (Diary, par. 401)

- "On the other hand, even these great graces are a burden for me, and I am barely able to carry them. I see my superiors' disbelief and doubts of all kinds and, for this reason, their apprehensive behavior toward me." (Diary, par. 786)

- "This is a grave and common defect in religious life; namely, that when one sees a suffering soul, one always want to add even more suffering. I do not say that everyone acts like this, but there are some." (Diary, par. 117)

- "I learned that certain people have a special gift for vexing others. They try you as best they can. The poor soul that falls into their hands can do nothing right; her best efforts are maliciously criticized." (Diary, par. 182)

- "I have been submitted to some tests at which I have had to laugh." (Diary, par. 112)

- "It often happens when one is ill, as in the case of Job in the Old testament, that as long as one can move about and work, everything is fine and dandy; but when God sends illness, somehow or other, there are fewer friends about. But yet, there are some. They still take interest in our suffering and all that, but if God sends a longer illness, even those faithful friends slowly begin to desert us. They visit us less frequently, and often their visits cause suffering. Instead of comforting us, they reproach us about certain things, which is an occasion of a good deal of suffering. And so the soul, like Job, is alone; but fortunately, it is not alone, because Jesus-Host is with it. After having tasted the above sufferings and spent a whole night in bitterness, the next morning, when the chaplain [Father Theodore] brought me Holy Communion, I had to control myself by sheer effort of will to keep from crying out at the top of my voice, 'Welcome, my true and only Friend.' Holy Communion gives me strength to suffer and fight." (Diary, par. 1509)

- "When I complained to the Lord Jesus about a certain person [saying], 'Jesus, how can this person pass judgment like that, even about an intention?' the Lord answered, Do not be surprised. That soul does not even know her own self, so how could she pass a fair judgment on another soul?" (Diary, par. 1528)

- "Oh, how painfully an ironic smile wounds, especially when one [appears to] speak with great sincerity." (Diary, par. 662)

- "Another thing: when sisters visit the sick, they should not ask in detail every time, 'What is hurting you, and how does it hurt?' because it is very tiresome to keep telling each sister the same thing about oneself. And it sometimes happens that one must repeat the same thing over and over many times a day." (Diary, par. 1555)

- "Today I felt bad that a week had gone by and no one had come to visit me. When I complained to the Lord, He answered, Isn't it enough for you that I visit you every day? I apologized to the Lord and the hurt vanished. O God, my strength, You are sufficient for me." (Diary, par. 827)

- "This is just one example among many. Sometimes it would seem that a sister of the second choir is made of stone, but she also is human and has a heart and feelings..." (Diary, par. 1510)

- "I am greatly surprised at how one can be so jealous. When I see someone else's good, I rejoice at it as if it were mine. The joy of others is my joy, and the suffering of others is my suffering, for otherwise I would not dare to commune with the Lord Jesus." (Diary, par. 633)

- "When I fell ill and was taken to the infirmary, I suffered much unpleasantness because of this. There were two of us sick in the infirmary. Sisters would come to see Sister N., but no one came to visit me. It is true that there was only one infirmary, but each one had her own cell. The winter nights were long, and Sister N. had the light and the radio headphones, while I could not even prepare my meditation for lack of a light. When nearly two weeks had passed in this way, I complained to the Lord one evening that I was suffering so much and that I could not even prepare my meditation because there was no light. And the Lord said that He would come every evening and give me the points for the next days meditation." (Diary, par. 149)

- "I have armed myself with patience in order to explain to each sister why I was not able to stay there: that is, because my health had become worse, even though I knew very well that certain sisters would inquire, not out of sympathy for my sufferings, but in order to add to them." (Diary, par. 1236)

- "I don't know how this happens, but the room in which I have been lying has been very much neglected. Sometimes, it has not been cleaned for more than two weeks. Often, no one would light a fire in the stove, and so my cough would get worse. Sometimes I would ask to have a fire lit, and at other times I did not have the courage to ask. On one occasion, when Mother Superior [Irene] came to see me and asked me if perhaps it was necessary to heat the room more, I said, No, because it was already getting warmer outside, and we had the window open." (Diary, par. 1649)

- "Once again, I am feeling worse today. A high fever is beginning to consume me, and I cannot take any food. I would like to have something refreshing to drink, but there is not even any water in my pitcher. All this, O Jesus, to obtain mercy for souls." (Diary, par. 1647) *[She is able to write so much, but she is not able to acquire water?]*

- "A certain sister is constantly persecuting me for the sole reason that God communes with me so intimately, and she thinks that this is all pretense on my part. When she thinks that I have done something amiss she says, 'Some people have revelations, but commit such faults!' She has said this to all the sisters and always in a derogatory sense, in order to make me out as some sort of an oddity. One day, it caused me much pain to think that this insignificant drop which is the human brain can so easily scrutinize the gifts of God. After Holy Communion, I prayed that the Lord would enlighten her, but nevertheless I learned that this soul will not attain perfection if she does not change her interior dispositions." (Diary, par. 1527)

- "Thus I have already been judged from all sides. There is no longer anything in me that has escaped the sisters. judgment. But it seems now to have worn itself out, and they have begun to leave me in peace. My tormented soul has had some rest, and I have learned that the Lord has been closest to me in times of such persecutions. This [truce] lasted for only a short time. A violent storm broke out again. And now the old suspicions became, for them, as if true facts, and once again I had to listen to the same old songs." (Diary, par. 128)

- "O my Jesus, when someone is unkind and unpleasant toward us, it is difficult enough to bear this kind of suffering. But this is very little in comparison to a suffering which I cannot bear; namely, that which I experience when someone exhibits kindness towards me and then lays snares at my feet at every step" (Diary, par. 1241)

- "Today I felt more ill, but Jesus has given me many more opportunities on this day to practice virtue. It so happened that I was busier than usual, and the sister in charge of the kitchen made it clear to me how irritated she was that I had come late for dinner, although it was quite impossible for me to have come sooner. At any rate, I felt so unwell that I had to ask Mother Superior to allow me to lie down. I went to ask

Sister N. to take my place, and again I got a scolding: 'What is this, Sister, you're so exhausted that you're going back to bed again! Confound you with all this lying in bed!' I put up with all that, but that wasn't the end. I still had to ask the sister who was in charge of the sick to bring me my meal. When I told her this, she burst out of the chapel into the corridor after me to give me a piece of her mind: 'Why on earth are you going to bed, Sister, etc...' I asked her not to bother bringing me anything. I am writing all this very briefly because it is not my intention to write about such things, and I am doing so merely to dissuade souls from treating others in this way, for this is displeasing to the Lord. In a suffering soul we should see Jesus Crucified, and not a loafer or burden on the community. A soul who suffers with submission to the will of God draws down more blessings on the whole convent than all the working sisters. Poor indeed is a convent where there are no sick sisters. God often grants many and great graces out of regard for the soul who are suffering, and He withholds many punishments solely because of the suffering souls." (Diary, par. 1268)

- "When I was alone, I tried to get up, but I was seized again with sickness, and so I stayed in bed with a calm conscience. Yet my heart had plenty to offer the Lord, joining itself spiritually to Him during the second Mass. After the second Mass, Sister Infirmarian returned to me, but this time in her capacity as infirmarian, and with a thermometer. But I had no fever, although I was seriously ill and unable to rise. So there was another sermon to tell me that I should not capitulate to illness. I answered her that I knew that here one was regarded as seriously ill only when one was in one's last agony. However, knowing that she was about to give me a lecture, I replied that at the present time I was in no need of being incited to greater zeal. And once again, I remained alone in my cell. My heart was crushed with sorrow, and bitterness flooded my soul, and I repeated these words: 'Welcome New Year; welcome, cup of bitterness.'" (Diary, par. 1453)

- "As usual, sisters from various houses came to the retreat. One of the sisters whom I had not seen for a long time, came to me cell and said she had something to tell me. I did not answer her, and she saw that I did not want to break silence. She said to me, 'I didn't know you were such an eccentric, sister,' and she went away. I was well aware that she had no other business with me than to satisfy her own curious self-love, O God, preserve me in faithfulness." (Diary, par. 171)

- "But some sisters seemed to find pleasure in vexing me in whatever way they could." (Diary, par. 126)

- "I can see now that there are few such priests who understand the full depth of God's work in the soul." (Diary, par. 234)

- "As soon as I left the chapel, I had an encounter with reality. I do not want to describe the details, but there was as much of it as I was able to bear. I would not have been able to bear even one drop more." (Diary, par. 190)

- "I could now see that everywhere I was being watched like a thief: in the chapel; while I was carrying out my duties; in my cell. I was now aware that, besides the presence of God, I had always close to me a human presence as well. And I must say that, more than once, this human presence bothered me greatly. There were times when I wondered whether I should undress to wash myself or not. Indeed, even that poor bed of mine was checked many times. More than once I was seized with laughter when I learned they would not even leave my bed alone. One of the sisters herself told me that she came to observe me in my cell every evening to see how I behave in it. Still, superiors are always superiors. And although they humiliated me personally and, on occasions, filled me with all kinds of doubts, they always allowed me to do what the Lord demanded." (Diary, par. 128)

- "During Holy Mass, I came to know that a certain priest does not effect much in souls because he thinks about himself and so is alone. God's grace takes flight; he relies on trifling external things, which have no importance in the eyes of God; and, being proud, he fritters away his time, wearing himself out to no purpose." (Diary, par. 1719) *[How could she know this? Why would God disclose such things to her if that is what is claimed?]*

She is also critical of some confessors and takes it upon herself to give advice to them! (see Diary, par. 112)

+ + +

Furthermore, when people agree with her or when things go her way, she tends to offer praise (or claim that God praises them or that they were enlightened by God or are speaking for God). For example, she says the following when things go her way with a certain priest and when a priest supports her work...

"Today during confession, the Lord Jesus spoke to me through the lips of a certain priest. This priest did not know my soul, and I only accused myself of my sins; yet he spoke these words to me: 'Accomplish faithfully everything that Jesus asks of you, despite the difficulties. Know that, although people may be angry with you, Jesus is not angry and never will be angry with you[!]. Pay no attention to human opinion.' This instruction surprised me at first; but I understood that the Lord was speaking through him without his realizing it. O holy mystery, what great treasures are contained in you! O holy faith, you are my guidepost!" (Diary, par. 763)

"I see Father Sopocko, how his mind is busily occupied and working in God's cause in order to present the wishes of God to the officials of the Church. As a result of his efforts, a new light will shine in the Church of God for the consolation of souls. Although for the present his soul is filled with bitterness, as though that were to be the reward for his efforts in the cause of the Lord, this will not however be the case. I see his joy, which nothing will diminish. God will grant him some of this joy already here on earth. I have never before come upon such great faithfulness to God as distinguishes this soul." (Diary, par. 1390)

But when people don't agree with her or when things don't go her way, she may be critical. For example...

"Once, when I saw that God had tried a certain Archbishop [Jalbrzykowski] because he was opposed to the cause and distrustful of it, I felt sorry for him and pleaded with God for him, and God relieved his suffering. God is very displeased with lack of trust in Him" (Diary, par. 595)

It seems rather convenient that Jesus always seems to be happy with persons that are like minded with her and displeased with those who are not!

+ + +

Also, we see that Faustina speaks with confidence of her own salvation...

- "And I sense my eternal destiny in heaven." (Diary, par. 1653)

- "I look forward with joy to the last stroke the Divine Artist will trace on my soul, which will give my soul a unique beauty that will distinguish me from the beauty of other souls. O great day, on which divine love will be confirmed in me. On that day, for the first time, I shall sing before heaven and earth the song of the Lord's fathomless mercy. This is my work and the mission which the Lord has destined for me from the beginning of the world." (Diary, par. 825)

- "I came before the throne of God. I saw a great and inaccessible light, and I saw a place destined for me, close to God. But what it was like I do not know, because a cloud covered it. However, my Guardian Angel said to me, 'Here is your throne, for your faithfulness in fulfilling the will of God.'" (Diary, par. 683)

- "I will commit my soul into the hands of the Heavenly Father, full of trust in Your unfathomable mercy. And when I stand at the foot of Your throne, the first hymn that I will sing will be one to Your mercy. Poor earth, I will not forget you. Although I feel that I will be immediately drowned in God as in an ocean of happiness, that will not be an obstacle to my returning to earth to encourage souls and incite them to trust in God's mercy" (Diary, par. 1582)

- "We know each other mutually, O Lord, in the dwelling of my heart. Yes, now it is I who am receiving You as a Guest in the little home of my heart, but the time is coming when You will call me to Your dwelling place, which You have prepared for me from the beginning of the world." (Diary, par. 909)

- "Today, one of the sisters [probably Sister Amelia] came to see me and said, 'Sister, I have a strange feeling, as though something were telling me to come to you and commend to you certain problems of mine before you die, and that perhaps you will able to beseech the Lord Jesus and arrange these things for me. Something keeps telling me that you will be able to obtain this for me.' I answered her with equal frankness that, yes, I felt in my soul that after my death I would be able to obtain more from the Lord Jesus than at the present time. 'I will remember you, Sister, before His throne.'" (Diary, par. 1614)

- "And when I stand at the foot of Your throne, the first hymn that I will sing will be one to Your mercy. Poor earth, I will not forget you. Although I feel that I will be immediately drowned in God as in an ocean of happiness, that will not be an obstacle to my returning to earth to encourage souls and incite them to trust in God's mercy. Indeed, this immersion in God will give me the possibility of boundless action." (Diary, par. 1582)

Yet the great St. Paul expresses in Scripture that even he was not certain regarding his own salvation...

- 1 Cor. 4:3-4: "It does not concern me in the least that I be judged by you or any human tribunal; I do not even pass judgment on myself; I am not conscious of anything against me, but I do not thereby stand acquitted; the one who judges me is the Lord."

- 1 Cor. 9:26-27: "Thus I do not run aimlessly; I do not fight as if I were shadowboxing. No, I drive my body and train it, for fear that, after having preached to others, I myself should be disqualified."

- Phil. 3:8 -14: "More than that, I even consider everything as a loss because of the supreme good of knowing Christ Jesus my Lord. For his sake I have accepted the loss of all things and I consider them so much rubbish, that I may gain Christ and be found in him, not having any righteousness of my own based on the law but that which comes through faith in Christ, the righteousness from God, depending on faith to know him and the power of his resurrection and the sharing of his sufferings by being conformed to his death, if somehow I may attain the resurrection from the dead. It is not that I have already taken hold of it or have already attained perfect maturity, but I continue my pursuit in hope that I may possess it, since I have indeed been taken possession of by Christ Jesus. Brothers, I for my part do not consider myself to have taken possession. Just one thing: forgetting what lies behind but straining forward to what lies ahead, I continue my pursuit toward the goal, the prize of God's upward calling, in Christ Jesus."

+ + +

And Faustina expresses a number of grandiose thoughts / desires / visions ...

- "I feel interiorly as if I were responsible for all souls." (Diary, par. 1505)

- "I would like to prepare all nations for the coming of the Word Incarnate." (Diary, par. 793)

- "Lord, I feel that I am going to remove the veil of heaven so that earth will not doubt Your goodness." (Diary, par. 483)

- "It seems to me that the whole world serves me and depends on me." (Diary, par. 195)

- "I sensed that I had a heart so big that nothing would be capable of filling it." (Diary, par. 15)

- "At such moments I have the feeling that the whole world is depending on me." (Diary, par. 870)

- "And although I am weak and small, You grant me the grace of Your omnipotence." (Diary, par. 2)

- "God gave me to know the greatness of my destiny" (Diary, par. 1410)

- "I felt that everything that existed was exclusively mine" (Diary, par. 1279)

- "in this state I suddenly feel that all the things God has, all the goods and treasures, are mine" (Diary, par. 454)

- "O my God, I have come to know that I am not of this earth; You, O Lord, have poured this profound awareness into my soul. My communion is more with heaven than with earth" (Diary, par. 107)

- "[The voice said to her,] Know that you are now on a great stage where all heaven and earth are watching you." (Diary, par. 1760)

- "I would like to be a priest, for then I would speak without cease about Your mercy to sinful souls drowned in despair. I would like to be a missionary and carry the light of faith to savage nations in order to make You known to souls, and to be completely consumed for them and to die a martyr's death, just as You died for them and for me." (Diary, par. 302)

- "O my God, I am conscious of my mission in the Holy Church." (Diary, par. 482)

- "I want to give You worship on behalf of all creatures and all inanimate creation; I call on the whole universe to glorify Your mercy" (Diary, par. 1749)

- "I know that I live, not for myself, but for a great number of souls." (Diary, par. 382)

- "This deeper knowledge of God gives me full liberty and spiritual freedom, and nothing can disturb my close union with Him, not even the angelic powers. I feel that I am great when I am united to God." (Diary, par. 1135)

- "In eternal happiness, I will not forget those on earth, I will obtain God's mercy for all[!]" (Diary, par. 1653)

- "How wondrously Jesus defends me; truly this is a great grace of God which I have experienced for a long time now." (Diary, par. 600)

- "The interior of my soul is like a large and magnificent world in which God and I live." (Diary, par. 582)

- "I know that whatever I ask of the Lord he will not refuse me, and He will give them that for which I ask." (Diary, par. 676)

- "I desire toil and suffering; let everything You have planned before the ages be fulfilled in me, O my Creator and Lord!" (Diary, par. 761)

- "And the blood of the Apostles boiled up within me. I will not be stingy with it; I will shed it all to the last drop for immortal souls." (Diary, par. 1249)

- "I desire to go throughout the whole world and speak to souls about the great mercy of God. Priests, help me [!] in this" (Diary, par. 491)

- "I am a host in Your hand, O Judge and Savior. In the last hour of my life, May the omnipotence of Your grace lead me to my goal, May Your compassion on the vessel of mercy become famous." (Diary, par. 1629)

- "I am going forward through life amidst rainbows and storms, but with my head held high with pride, for I am a royal child. I feel that the blood of Jesus is circulating in my veins" (Diary, par. 992)

- "When I rose to do battle, an inexperienced knight, I felt I had a knight's blood, though still a child" (Diary, par. 1654)

- "There are moments when Jesus gives me knowledge within my soul, and then everything that exists on earth is at my service: friends, enemies, success, adversity... All things, willing or not, must serve me." (Diary, par. 1720)

- "Then, in an instant, I was caught up to stand near Jesus, and I stood on the altar [!] next to the Lord Jesus, and my spirit was filled with happiness so great that I am unable to comprehend it or write about it. A profound peace as well as repose filled my soul. Jesus bent toward me and said with great kindness, What is it you desire, My daughter? And I answered, 'I desire worship and glory be given to Your mercy.' I already am receiving worship by the institution and celebration of this Feast; what else do you desire? I then looked at the immense crowd worshiping The Divine Mercy and I said to the Lord, 'Jesus, bless all those who are gathered to give glory to You and to venerate Your infinite mercy.' Jesus made a sign of the cross with His hand, and this blessing was reflected in the souls like a flash of light." (Diary, par. 1048)

- "Today, I saw two enormous pillars implanted in the ground; I had implanted one of them, and a certain person, S.M., the other. We had done so with unheard-of effort, much fatigue and difficulty. And when I had implanted the pillar, I myself wondered where such extraordinary strength had come from, And I recognized that I had not done this by my own strength, but with the power which came from above. These two pillars were close to each other, in the area of the image. And I saw the image, raised up very high and hanging from these two pillars. In an instant, there stood a large temple, supported both from within and from without, upon these two pillars." (Diary, par. 1689)

+ + +

She also tends to write about her good deeds...

- "I often take upon myself the torments of our students." (Diary, par. 192)

- "you small, everyday sacrifices, you are to me like wild flowers which I strew over the feet of my beloved Jesus. I sometimes compare these trifles to the heroic virtues and that is because their enduring nature demands heroism." (Diary, par. 208)

- "The good God entrusted her to my care, and for two weeks I was able to work with her. But how many sacrifices this soul cost me is known only to God. For no other soul did I bring so many sacrifices and sufferings and prayers before the throne of God as I did for her soul. I felt that I had forced God to grant her grace." (Diary, par. 202)

- "What also cost me a lot was that I had to kiss the children. The women I knew came with their children and asked me to take them in my arms, at least for a moment, and kiss them. They regarded this as a great favor, and for me it was a chance to practice virtue, since many of the children were quite dirty. To overcome my feelings and show no repugnance, I would kiss such a dirty child twice. Once of these friends came with a child whose eyes were diseased and filled with pus, and she said to me, 'Sister, take it in your arms for a moment, please.' My nature recoiled, but not paying attention to anything, I took the child and kissed it twice, right on the infection, asking God to heal it." (Diary, par. 401)

- "My country, how much you cost me! There is no day in which I do not pray for you." (Diary, par. 1188)

- "Jesus always found silence in my heart, although it sometimes cost me a lot." (Diary, par. 185)

- "Once, when I returned to my cell, I was so tired that I had to rest a moment before I started to undress, and when I was already undressed, one of the sisters asked me to fetch her some hot water. Although I was tired, I dressed quickly and brought her the water she wanted, even though it was quite a long walk from the cell to the kitchen, and the mud was ankle-deep." (Diary, par. 285)

- "Today I wore a chain belt for seven hours in order to obtain the grace of repentance for that soul." (Diary, par. 1248)

- Etc.

Yet scripture says our good deeds should be kept in secret...

> Mt. 6:1-4: "But take care not to perform righteous deeds in order that people may see them; otherwise, you will have no recompense from your heavenly Father. When you give alms, do not blow a trumpet before you, as the hypocrites do in the synagogues and in the streets to win the praise of others. Amen, I say to you, they have received their reward. But when you give alms, do not let your left hand know what your right is doing, so that your almsgiving may be secret. And your Father who sees in secret will repay you."

+ + +

Faustina also writes about her sufferings and her (so-called) 'martyrdom' in which no drop of blood is shed (she even claims Jesus made a reference to her "silent day-to-day martyrdom" in par. 1184)...

- "Today I was cleaning the room of one of the sisters. Although I was trying to clean it with utmost care, she kept following me all the time and saying, 'You've left a speck of dust here and a spot on the floor there.' At each of her remarks I did each place over a dozen times just to satisfy her. It is not work that makes me tired, but all this talking and excessive demands. My whole day's martyrdom was not enough for her, so she went to the Directress and complained, 'Mother, who is this careless sister who doesn't know how to work quickly?' The next day, I went again to do the same job, without trying to explain myself. When she started driving me, I thought, 'Jesus, one can be a silent martyr; it is not the work that wears you out, but this kind of martyrdom.'" (Diary, par. 181)

- "From early morning, today, a strange power has been pushing me to action, not giving me a moment's peace. A strange ardor has been lit in my heart, urging me to action, and I cannot stop it. This is a secret martyrdom known only to God" (Diary, par. 569)

- "During the morning meditation, I felt an aversion and a repugnance for all created things. Everything pales before my eyes; my spirit is detached from all things. I desire only God Himself, and yet I must live. This is a martyrdom beyond description." (Diary, par. 856)

- "God alone knows what I put up with, day and night. It seems to me that the worst torments of the martyrs would be easier for me to bear than what I am going through, though without the shedding of a drop of blood." (Diary, par. 1263)

- "No one can understand or comprehend, nor can I myself describe, my torments. But there can be no sufferings greater than this. The sufferings of the martyrs are not greater because, at such times, death would be a relief for me. There is nothing to which I can compare these sufferings, this endless agony of the soul." (Diary, par. 1116)

Talk about making light of the horrific & inconceivable sufferings that the real martyrs went through!

+ + +

Faustina also indicates her desire to become a "great saint"...

"My Jesus, You know that from my earliest years I have wanted to become a great saint" (Diary, par. 1372)

And claims that Jesus even called her a saint...

- "When I took the Messenger of the Sacred Heart into my hand and read the account of the canonization of Saint

Andrew Bobola, my soul was instantly filled with a great longing that our Congregation, too, might have a saint, and I wept like a child that there was no saint in our midst. And I said to the Lord, 'I know Your generosity, and yet it seems to me that You are less generous toward us.' And I began again to weep like a little child. And the Lord Jesus said to me, Don't cry. You are that saint." (Diary, par. 1650)

- "And I began to complain to the Lord Jesus, asking why this should be so, and the Lord answered me, Are you sad because of this? Of course you are a saint." (Diary, par. 1571)

+ + +

She furthermore claims she kept the 'virginity' of her heart and soul intact...

"God gave me the inner knowledge that I had never lost my innocence, and that despite all dangers in which I had found myself, He Himself had been guarding me so that the virginity of my soul and heart would remain intact" (Diary, par. 1095)

...even though she admits to misrepresenting herself "often" at the beginning of religious life...

"I often represented myself to my superiors other than I was in reality and spoke of miseries of which I had no notion." (Diary, par. 1503)

And this even though she admits to participating in a seemingly sacrilegious confession and a forced baptism of adult Jewish woman...

"A certain person seems to have made it her task to try out my virtue in all sorts of ways. One day, she stopped me in the corridor and began by saying that she had no grounds for rebuking me, but she ordered me to stand there opposite the small chapel for half an hour and to wait for Mother Superior, who was to pass by there after recreation, and I was to accuse myself of various things which she had told me to say. Although I had no idea of these things being on my soul, I was obedient and waited for Mother Superior for a full half hour. Each sister who passed by looked at me with a smile. When I accused myself before Mother Superior [Raphael], she sent me to my confessor. When I made my confession, the priest saw immediately that this was something that did not come from my own soul and that I had not the faintest idea of such things. He was very surprised that this person had dared to take upon herself to give such orders." (Diary, par. 196)

[Reminder: It is wrong to confess sins that you didn't commit, and may even be sacrilegious ("violation or misuse of what is regarded as sacred"). Also, we must have sorrow for all sins committed. As the Catechism of St. Pius X, "If one confesses only venial sins without having sorrow for at least one of them, his confession is in vain; moreover it would be sacrilegious if the absence of sorrow was conscious."]

And...

"This day is so special for me; even though I encountered so many sufferings, my soul is overflowing with great joy. In a private room next to mine, there was a Jewish woman who was seriously ill. I went to see her three days ago and was deeply pained at the thought that she would soon die without having her soul cleansed by the grace of Baptism. I had an understanding with her nurse, a [religious] Sister, that when her last moment would be approaching, she would baptize her. There was this difficulty however, that there were always some Jewish people with her. However, I felt inspired to pray before the image which Jesus had instructed me to have painted. I have a leaflet with the Image of the divine Mercy on the cover. And I said to the Lord, 'Jesus, You Yourself told me that You would grant many graces through this image. I ask You, then, for the grace of Holy Baptism for this Jewish lady. It makes no difference who will baptize her, as long as she is baptized.'

After these words, I felt strangely at peace, and I was quite sure that, despite the difficulties, the waters of Holy Baptism would be poured upon her soul. That night, when she was very low, I got out of bed three times to see her, watching for the right moment to give her this grace. The next morning, she seemed to feel a little better. In the afternoon her last moment began to approach. The Sister who was her nurse said that Baptism would be difficult because they were with her. The moment came when the sick woman began to lose consciousness, and as a result, in order to save her, they began to run about; some [went] to fetch the doctor, while others went off in other directions to find help.

And so the patient was left alone, and Sister baptized her, and before they had all rushed back, her soul was beautiful, adorned with God's grace. Her final agony began immediately, but it did not last long. It was as if she fell asleep. All of a sudden, I saw her soul ascending to heaven [!] in wondrous beauty. Oh, how beautiful is a soul with sanctifying grace! Joy flooded my heart that before this image I had received so great a grace for this soul.

Oh, how great is God's mercy; let every soul praise it. O my Jesus, that soul for all eternity will be singing You a hymn of mercy. I shall not forget the impression this day has made on my soul. This is the second great grace which I have received here for souls before this image.

Oh, how good the Lord is, and how full of compassion;
Jesus, how heartily I thank You for these graces."
(Diary, par. 916-917)

Some notes concerning the above:

- **It is not licit to unconditionally baptize an adult who has had use of their faculties and who has not indicated a desire to be baptized**

- **Faustina must have sensed that this was wrong or else they wouldn't have had to do it 'sneakily' when the other Jews left the room** (also they would hopefully have known to call a priest to do the baptism if they knew it was licit for the woman to be baptized)

- **Faustina wrongly writes as if what was done was a good thing and shows no repentance for her part in it** (she actually shows the opposite sentiments!)

- **It is against Church teaching to forcibly baptize adults without their consent**. As the Catechism of the Council of Trent states, "The faithful are also to be instructed in the necessary dispositions for Baptism. In the first place they must desire and intend to receive it; for as in Baptism we all die to sin and resolve to live a new life, it is fit that it be administered to those only who receive it of their own free will and accord; it is to be forced upon none. Hence we learn from holy tradition that it has been the invariable practice to administer Baptism to no (adult) individual without previously asking him if he be willing to receive it."

- **She wrongly claims that the sacrament had its effect and saved the woman**, yet the Catechism of the Council of Trent states: "Besides a wish to be baptized, in order to obtain the grace of the Sacrament, faith is also necessary. Our Lord and Savior has said: He that believes and is baptized shall be saved." As Mk. 16:15-16 states, "[Jesus] said to them, 'Go into the whole world and proclaim the gospel to every creature. Whoever believes and is baptized will be saved; whoever does not believe [!] will be condemned.'" Jesus requires both faith AND baptism -- and the baptism is to be consensual, not forced!

- **Faustina attributes this illicit baptism to graces obtained when she prayed before the image. (So what does that say about the supposed graces she claims people receive when they pray before the image?) Most offensively, she is essentially implying it was God's grace that resulted in an illicit baptism!**

- **In light of the above (e.g. "Joy flooded my heart that before this image I had received so great a grace for this soul" and "I saw her soul ascending to heaven in wondrous beauty"), how are we to trust Faustina's claimed visions or her theology? Faustina actually claims she saw the woman's soul ascending to heaven! She appears to have no clue that what was done was wrong or that the forced baptism would have no effect! Yet she claims all this special knowledge from God!**

- **The Church should issue a clear condemnation of this action, especially since this devotion is being so heavily promoted today.**

+ + +

Faustina also feels that God "cannot be happy" without her...

"I do not know how to live without God, but I also feel that God, absolutely self-sufficient though He is, cannot be happy without me" (Diary, par. 1120)

+ + +

And she claims a special mission from God...

- "my God, I am conscious of my mission in the Holy Church" (Diary, par. 482)

- Jesus supposedly said, "I am giving you a share in the redemption of mankind." (Diary, par. 310)

- "Glorifying Your mercy is the exclusive task of my life." (Diary, par. 1242)

- "Then I heard these words in my soul: Your purpose and that of your companions is to unite yourselves with Me as closely as possible; through love You will reconcile earth with heaven, you will soften the just anger of God, and you will plead for mercy for the world." (Diary, par. 531)

- She claims Jesus said, "My daughter, secretary of My mercy, your duty is not only to write about and proclaim My mercy, but also to beg for this grace for them" (Diary, par. 1160)

- And: "You are the secretary of My mercy. I have chosen you for that office in this life and the next life." (Diary, par. 1605)

- "Jesus said, My daughter give Me souls. Know that it is your mission to win souls for Me by prayer and sacrifice, and by encouraging them to trust in My mercy." (Diary, par. 1690)

- "On that day, for the first time, I shall sing before heaven and earth the song of the Lord's fathomless mercy. This is my work and the mission which the Lord has destined for me from the beginning of the world" (Diary, par. 825)

- "I presented to the director of my soul the fear that seized me because of this mission for which God was using me..." (Diary, par. 331)

- "I heard these words: By your entreaties, you and your companions shall obtain mercy for yourselves and for the world." (Diary, par. 435)

- "fight for the salvation of souls, exhorting them to trust in My mercy, as that is your task in this life and in the life to come." (Diary, par. 1452)

- The Blessed Virgin Mary supposedly said, "as for you, you have to speak to the world about His great mercy and prepare the world for the Second Coming" (Diary, par. 635)

- "O most sweet Jesus, who have graciously demanded that I tell the whole world of Your incomprehensible mercy, this day I take into my hands the two rays that spring from Your merciful Heart; that is, the Blood and the Water; and I scatter them all over the globe so that each soul may receive Your mercy and, having received it, may glorify it for endless ages. O most sweet Jesus who, in Your incomprehensible kindness, have deigned to unite my wretched heart to Your most merciful Heart, it is with Your own Heart that I glorify God, our Father, as no soul has ever glorified Him before." (Diary, par. 836)

- She claims she "heard these words": "In the Old Covenant I sent prophets wielding thunderbolts to My People. Today I am sending you with My mercy to the people of the whole world." (Diary, par. 1588) *[Is she not essentially claiming here that she is a post-New Testament prophet?!]*

- "Then I heard a voice: Apostle [!] of My mercy, proclaim to the whole world My unfathomable mercy." (Diary, par. 1142)

- "I suddenly saw the Lord Jesus, radiant wish unspeakable beauty, and He said to me with kindness, My chosen one, I will give you even greater graces that you may be the witness of My infinite mercy throughout all eternity." (Diary, par. 400)

- "You are a witness of My mercy. You shall stand before My throne forever as a living witness to My mercy." (Diary, par. 417)

- "Your assignment and duty here on earth is to beg for mercy for the whole world." (Diary, par. 570)

- "Tell the world about My mercy and My love." (Diary, par. 1074)

- "Speak to the whole world about My mercy." (Diary, par. 1190)

- "When I became aware of God's great plans for me, I was frightened at their greatness and felt myself quite incapable of fulfilling them, and I began to avoid interior conversations with Him, filling up the time with vocal prayer. I did this out of humility, but I soon recognized it was not true humility, but rather a great temptation from the devil. When, on one occasion, instead of interior prayer, I took up a book of spiritual reading, I heard these words spoken distinctly and forcefully within my soul, You will prepare the world for My final coming. These words moved me deeply, and although I pretended not to hear them, I understood them very well and had no doubt about them. Once, being tired out from this battle of love with God, and making constant excuses on the grounds that I was unable to carry out this task, I wanted to leave the chapel, but some force held me back and I found myself powerless. Then I heard these words, You intend to leave the chapel, but you shall not get away from Me, for I am everywhere. You cannot do anything of yourself, but with Me you can do all things." (Diary, par. 429)

+ + +

She claims she is even tasked with instructing her superiors and priests...

- "I heard these words: Tell the Superior that I want adoration to take place here for the intention of imploring mercy for the world." (Diary, par. 1070)

- "Tell My priests that hardened sinners will repent on hearing their words when they speak about My unfathomable mercy, about the compassion I have for them in My Heart." (Diary, par. 1521)

- "Jesus said to me, Go to Mother Superior and tell her that those two sisters are in danger of committing a mortal sin." (Diary, par. 43)

- "One morning I heard these words in my soul: Go to Mother General [Michael] and tell her that this thing displeases Me in such and such a house. I cannot mention what the thing was nor the house in question, but I did tell it to Mother General, although it cost me very much." (Diary, par. 191)

- "Today, the Lord said to me, Tell the Reverend Professor [probably Father Theodore] that I desire that on the Feast of My Mercy he deliver a sermon about My fathomless mercy. I fulfilled God's wish, but the priest did not want to acknowledge the Lord's message. When I left the confessional, I heard these words: Do as I tell you and be at peace; this matter is between him and Me. You will not be held responsible for this." (Diary, par. 1072)

- "My daughter, speak to priests about this inconceivable mercy of Mine." (Diary, par. 177)

- "A Blessed Mother of this type I had not yet seen. Then She looked at me kindly and said: I am the Mother of God of Priests. At that, She lowered Jesus from her arm to the ground, raised Her right hand heavenward and said: O God, bless Poland, bless priests. Then She addressed me once again: Tell the priests what you have seen." (Diary, par. 1585)

69

+ + +

Yet, despite her countless alleged mystical experiences, her grandiose thoughts, and her supposed mission, Faustina refers to her life as drab, humdrum...

- "Oh, how drab and full of misunderstandings is this life!" (Diary, par. 900)

- "my drab, everyday life" (Diary, par. 210)

- "life so dull and monotonous, how many treasures you contain!" (Diary, par. 62)

- "I feel that I have been totally imbued with God and, with this God, I am going back to my everyday life, so drab, tiresome and wearying," (Diary, par. 1363)

- "humdrum days, filled with darkness, I look upon you with a solemn and festive eye." (Diary, par. 1373)

How could any life supposedly so full of communication with Jesus and Mary ever be considered drab or humdrum?!

+ + +

And, unlike some other saints who miraculously emitted pleasant odors, she believes God assuaged her doubts by allowing her to smell like a corpse...

"One day, I began to doubt as to how it was possible to feel this continual decaying of the body and at the same time to be able to walk and work. Perhaps this was some kind of an illusion. Yet it cannot be an illusion, because it causes me such terrible pains. As I was thinking about this, one of the sisters came to converse with me. After a minute or two, she made a terribly wry face and said, 'Sister, I smell a corpse here, as though it were decaying.

70

O how dreadful it is!' I said to her, 'Do not be frightened, Sister, that smell of a corpse comes from me.' She was very surprised and said she could not stand it any longer. After she had gone, I understood that God had allowed her to sense this so that I would have no doubt, but that He was no less than miraculously keeping the knowledge of this suffering from the whole community. O my Jesus, only You know the full depth of this sacrifice." (Diary, par. 1430)

About the smell, she later comments...

"I feel the complete decay of my organism, Although I am still living and working. Death will be no tragedy for me, Because I have long felt it. Although it is very unpleasant for nature to constantly smell one's own corpse" (Diary, par. 1435)

+ + +

Furthermore, this supposed 'mission' that she claims to have is problematic for a number of reasons, for example...

- doctrinal problems with her message (see below)

- the idea that Jesus would call an 'Apostle' 1,900 years after His death to proclaim new doctrine is ludicrous, not to mentioned condemned [for example, see condemned error #21 in Lamentabili Sane, The Syllabus Condemning the Errors of the Modernists (see http://www.mycatholicsource.com/mcs/pd/lamentabili_sane.htm): "Revelation, constituting the object of the Catholic faith, was not completed with the (original, real) Apostles."). Our faith does not allow later additions - there is nothing Jesus 'forgot' to tell us when he was here!

- the feminist-pleasing idea that Jesus would call a woman 'Apostle' is contradictory to Scripture, Tradition, and Church teaching (for example, consider St. Paul's comment in 1 Tm. 2:12: "I do not permit a woman to teach or to have authority over a man. She must be quiet."). Especially considering the disobedient women in our time who cannot accept their God given roles, are we really to believe that God would pick a woman to 'teach the Church' and call her an 'Apostle'? *[Note: For more on this topic, try here: http://www.mycatholicsource.com/mcs/pc/vocations/top_reas ons_why_women_cant_be_priests.htm]*

Moreover, the idea that Faustina has an important 'mission' in the Church on earth seems to be contradicted in her very own writings, as she claims Jesus offered to make a new world for her to live in (where she would presumably no longer have a mission on earth as she would no longer even live on earth)...

"Once, I suddenly saw Jesus in great majesty, and He spoke these words to me: My daughter, if you wish, I will this instant create a new world, more beautiful than this one, and you will live there for the rest of your life." (Diary, par. 587)

This would certainly have put an end to her mission - how would she have accomplished her supposed 'mission' on earth if she lived in another world? Her 'mission' must not have been that important if Jesus offered to remove her from this world to go live there!

Also, let's not forget that the real Apostles... *[Note: See http://www.mycatholicsource.com/mcs/pcs/the_apostles.htm]*

- were all men

- were Bishops

- had Holy Orders (don't forget that there is a direct line of succession from the Apostles to today's bishops)

- lived during Jesus' time

- were given authority and power (Faustina does not have such authority or power!)

- spread the Catholic faith - not a message from a supposed 20th century apparition

- performed miracles personally

- were all martyred - except St. John who survived his attempted martyrdom (and martyrdom is meant here in the literal sense)

+ + +

Furthermore, much of her theology seems problematic. For example, besides the various points indicated above, consider the following...

» She claims that the Feast of Mercy God supposedly wanted is "the last hope of salvation" - and she also claims that those who do not adore God's mercy will "perish for all eternity"! Yet the annual feast of mercy is unnecessary [confession - the real 'last hope of salvation'! - is available every day, and even her version of the feast is essentially equivalent to a plenary indulgence - something that is available every day of the week (see http://www.mycatholicsource.com/mcs/cg/indulgences.htm)]. Furthermore, we cannot be required to adore God's mercy under penalty of hellfire based on a private revelation. This is an unheard of new 'mortal sin' and the Church CANNOT add to the deposit of faith that was passed on to the Apostles.

> "Jesus looked at me and said, Souls perish in spite of My bitter Passion. I am giving them the last hope of salvation; that is, the Feast of My Mercy. If they will not adore My mercy, they will perish for all eternity." (Diary, par. 965)

73

» She claims "ALL creatures, whether they know it or not, and whether they want to or not, ALWAYS fulfill My will" (Diary, par. 586, emphasis added). Tell that to rape victims concerning their perpetrators! Or to robbery victims! Or to abused children! Etc. Clearly, people act against God's will all the time. God allows evil things to happen (by His 'permissive will'), but that does NOT mean He positively wills evil.

» She says God "claim[s] veneration for My mercy from every creature", but this was unheard of for 1,900 years and the Church CANNOT add to the deposit of faith that was passed on to the Apostles. Furthermore, Scripture says that "mercy and anger alike are with him" (Sirach 5:7), so if we were actually required to venerate His mercy, shouldn't we also be required to venerate His anger? For that matter, where in Scripture does God specifically claim veneration for any of His attributes in particular?

> "I claim veneration for My mercy from every creature, but above all from you, since it is to you that I have given the most profound understanding of this mystery." (Diary, par. 1572)

» She claims a chaplet and novena supposedly dictated by Christ bring all sorts of special favors (see below). However, we must ask...

- Why did Christ wait 1,900 years to give us these 'important prayers' - why did He not leave such 'important prayers' along with the Lord's Prayer when he was walking the earth?

- Why would Christ tell us to pray these prayers for the dying instead of doing what Holy Scripture tells us to do (namely, get the priest to dispense the sacrament of extreme unction to the dying person)?

- How can a sinner be saved by another lay person's prayers if he does not repent of his own free will?

- How is it that the mere reciting of a chaplet - without any repentance required on the sinner's part - can supposedly mitigate God's anger? Wouldn't such a chaplet essentially be 'better than' or 'more effective than' confession since confession requires repentance? - Yet such a claim is ludicrous!

- How can a chaplet - not a sacrament - be someone's "last hope of salvation"?

- And why would a priest recommend praying a chaplet (derived from a private revelation) as someone's "last hope of salvation" - rather than recommending repentance & receiving grace-giving sacraments?

- Why did Jesus institute the sacrament of extreme unction if all that is needed is this chaplet?

- Why is this chaplet - which is said on rosary beads - so heavily promoted in her writings at the expense of the Rosary itself? We know that popes & saints - and even the Blessed Virgin Mary herself - have strongly recommended the Rosary in the clearest and strongest of terms.

- Why does her diary also seem to ignore other traditional forms of Catholic devotion with respect to the dying - e.g. praying to St. Joseph?

Some passages from her diary regarding the chaplet and novena...

- "When I entered my solitude, I heard these words: At the hour of their death, I defend as My own glory every soul that will say this chaplet; or when others say it for a dying person, the indulgence is the same. When this chaplet is said by the bedside of a dying person, God's anger is placated, unfathomable mercy envelops the soul, and the very depths of My tender mercy are moved for the sake of the sorrowful Passion of My Son." (Diary, par. 811)

- "When I came to myself, I understood how very important the chaplet was for the dying. It appeases the anger of God." (Diary, par. 1565)

- "The Lord told me to say this chaplet for nine days before the Feast of Mercy. It is to begin on Good Friday. By this novena, I will grant every possible grace to souls." (Diary, par. 796)

- "This chaplet mitigates God's anger, as He Himself told me." (Diary, par. 1036)

- "Once, as I was going down the hall to the kitchen, I heard these words in my soul: Say unceasingly the chaplet that I have taught you. Whoever will recite it will receive great mercy at the hour of death. Priests will recommend it to sinners as their last hope of salvation[!]. Even if there were a sinner most hardened, if he were to recite this chaplet only once, he would receive grace from My infinite mercy. I desire that the whole world know My infinite mercy. I desire to grant unimaginable graces to those souls who trust in My mercy." (Diary, par. 687)

- "The Lord's Promise: The souls that say this chaplet will be embraced by My mercy during their lifetime and especially at the hour of their death." (Diary, par. 754)

- "My daughter, encourage souls to say the chaplet which I have given to you. It pleases Me to grant everything they ask of Me by saying the chaplet. When hardened [!] sinners say it, I will fill their souls with peace, and the hour of their death will be a happy one." (Diary, par. 1541)

- "Write that when they say this chaplet in the presence of the dying, I will stand between My Father and the dying person, not as the just Judge but as the merciful Savior." (Diary, par. 1541)

- "When I looked at the plants, thirsting for the rain I was moved with pity, and I decided to say the chaplet until the Lord would send us rain. Before supper, the sky covered over with clouds, and a heavy rain fell on the earth. I had been saying this prayer without interruption for three hours. And the Lord let me know that everything can be obtained by means of this prayer." (Diary, par. 1128)

» She claims that Christ wanted her to pray for a dying person, rather than instructing someone to call a priest for the dying person (see http://www.mycatholicsource.com/mcs/pc/sacraments/extreme_unction.htm). Yet we must ask: How can a lay person praying a chaplet appease God's anger against someone else who is apparently not repentant for their sins? Why should she not do what Scripture says, namely call a priest, as indicated in Jms. 5:14-15: "Is anyone among you sick? He should summon the presbyters (priests) of the church, and they should pray over him and anoint (him) with oil in the name of the Lord, and the prayer of faith will save the sick person, and the Lord will raise him up. If he has committed any sins, he will be forgiven."

"When I entered the chapel for a moment, the Lord said to me, My daughter, help Me to save a certain dying sinner. Say the chaplet that I have taught you for him. When I began to say the chaplet, I saw the man dying in the midst of terrible torment and struggle. His Guardian Angel was defending him, but he was, as it were, powerless against the enormity of the soul's misery. A multitude of devils was waiting for the soul. But while I was saying the chaplet, I saw Jesus just as He is depicted in the image. The rays which issued from Jesus. Heart enveloped the sick man, and the powers of darkness fled in panic. The sick man peacefully breathed his last. When I came to myself, I understood how very important the chaplet was for the dying. It appeases the anger of God." (Diary, par. 1565)

» **Despite Catholic teaching to the contrary, her diary gives the impression that sinners can attain justification on their own - e.g. by approaching God's 'sea of mercy' - apparently without need of baptism, confession, or even repentance. It also wrongly indicates that those who simply 'trust' in Mercy will receive graces and be saved - rather than those who repent and receive the sacraments.**

- "Tell souls that from this fount of mercy souls draw graces solely [!] with the vessel of trust." (Diary, par. 1602) *[Note: Vessel of trust rather than true sorrow for sin!]*

- "The graces of My mercy are drawn by means of one vessel only [!], and that is – trust. The more a soul trusts, the more it will receive." (Diary, par. 1578)

- "Today the Lord said to me, I have opened My Heart as a living fountain of mercy. Let all souls draw life from it. Let them approach this sea of mercy with great trust. Sinners will attain justification, and the just will be confirmed in good. Whoever places his trust in My mercy will be filled with My divine peace at the hour of death." (Diary, par. 1520)

» **She makes the surprising claim that Jesus said it was better for a priest to have spent his time proclaiming 'the worship of God's mercy' (something that does not even require Holy Orders) rather than actually dispensing mercy in the confessional (something only priests can do)!**

"[August] 30. Reverend Father Sopocko left this morning. When I was steeped in a prayer of thanksgiving for the great grace that I had received from God; namely, that of seeing Father, I became united in a special way with the Lord who said to me, He is a priest after My own Heart; his efforts are pleasing to Me. You see, My daughter, that My will must be done and that which I had promised you, I shall do. Through him I spread comfort to suffering and careworn souls. Through him it pleased Me to proclaim the worship of My mercy. And through this work of mercy more souls will come close to Me than otherwise would have, even if he had kept giving absolution day and night for the rest of his life, because by so doing, he would have labored only for as long as he lived; whereas, thanks to this work of mercy, he will be laboring till the end of the world." (Diary, par. 1256)

» She claims that God desires "that priests proclaim this great mercy of Mine towards souls of sinners" (Diary, par. 50), but why is it that God supposedly wants priests to speak of His great mercy when Jesus himself usually spoke of judgment rather than of mercy? Why is it that great preachers have said that it is sermons on hell (not mercy!) that produce conversions?

» She claims that God desires an annual feast of mercy [which she says was already in place, even though not well known at the time (see Diary, par. 341)], and it was later added to the Novus Ordo calendar, complete with a plenary indulgence. Yet, as indicated above, this annual feast that she describes was unnecessary. First of all, confession is already available every day (if not scheduled, then certainly by appointment) - and confession is THE 'tribunal of mercy'. Furthermore, her version of this feast is essentially equivalent to a plenary indulgence, and a plenary indulgence is also available every day of the week. So there was no need for this special feast that she claims God had so desired. Also, Faustina's Divine Mercy devotees' promotion of this feast - which falls the Sunday after Easter - can tend to overshadow the greatest of all feasts - Easter itself! Is it not ironic that the truly greatest feast concerning God's mercy to sinners - Easter Sunday - seems sometimes put in the background by Faustina's Divine Mercy devotees in favor of this lesser 'feast of mercy' (traditionally called 'low Sunday')? And let's not even get into the notion that she claims Christ offered a

direct plenary indulgence (a supposed 'second baptism') that wasn't at that time promulgated by His own Church.

- "I desire that the Feast of Mercy be a refuge and shelter for all souls, and especially for poor sinners. On that day the very depths of My tender mercy are open. I pour out a whole ocean of graces upon those souls who approach the Fount of My Mercy. The soul that will go to Confession and receive Holy Communion shall obtain complete forgiveness of sins and punishment. On that day all the divine floodgates through which graces flow are opened. Let no soul fear to draw near to Me, even though its sins be as scarlet [! - Yet, how would this be if the sinner already had a good confession?]. My mercy is so great that no mind, be it of man or of angel, will be able to fathom it throughout all eternity. Everything that exists has come forth from the very depths of My most tender mercy. Every soul in its relation to Me will contemplate My love and mercy throughout eternity. The Feast of Mercy emerged from My very depths of tenderness. It is My desire that it be solemnly celebrated on the first Sunday after Easter. Mankind will not have peace until it turns to the Fount of My Mercy." (Diary, par. 699)

- "tell the whole world of My great mercy; that whoever approaches the Fount of Life on this day will be granted complete remission of sins and punishment." (Diary, par. 300)

- "He spoke these words to me: I want to grant a complete pardon to the souls that will go to Confession and receive Holy Communion on the Feast of My mercy." (Diary, par. 1109)

» Despite the fact that God is absolutely perfect in all respects, she claims mercy is God's "greatest attribute"! (see below for more on this matter)

» She claims that "Only that soul who wants it will be damned, for God condemns no one" (Diary, par. 1452), but this is NOT what scripture says. Besides being dangerous theology, it seems to go against common sense. People may want to sin, but who "wants" to be dammed? How can there be a Just Judge if all He is doing is simply giving people what they desire? Also, in Jesus' parables, we see that some persons are damned who apparently didn't want to be damned...

Lk. 16:19-31: "There was a rich man who dressed in purple garments and fine linen and dined sumptuously each day. And lying at his door was a poor man named Lazarus, covered with sores, who would gladly have eaten his fill of the scraps that fell from the rich man's table. Dogs even used to come and lick his sores. When the poor man died, he was carried away by angels to the bosom of Abraham. The rich man also died and was buried, and from the netherworld, where he was in torment, he raised his eyes and saw Abraham far off and Lazarus at his side. And he cried out, 'Father Abraham, have pity on me. Send Lazarus to dip the tip of his finger in water and cool my tongue, for I am suffering torment in these flames.' Abraham replied, 'My child, remember that you received what was good during your lifetime while Lazarus likewise received what was bad; but now he is comforted here, whereas you are tormented. Moreover, between us and you a great chasm is established to prevent anyone from crossing who might wish to go from our side to yours or from your side to ours.' He said, 'Then I beg you, father, send him to my father's house, for I have five brothers, so that he may warn them, lest they too come to this place of torment.' But Abraham replied, 'They have Moses and the prophets. Let them listen to them.' He said, 'Oh no, father Abraham, but if someone from the dead goes to them, they will repent.' Then Abraham said, 'If they will not listen to Moses and the prophets, neither will they be persuaded if someone should rise from the dead.'"

Mt. 25:31-46: "When the Son of Man comes in his glory, and all the angels with him, he will sit upon his glorious throne, and all the nations will be assembled before him. And he will separate them one from another, as a shepherd separates the sheep from the goats. He will place the sheep on his right and the goats on his left. Then the king will say to those on his right, 'Come, you who are blessed by my Father. Inherit the kingdom prepared for you from the foundation of the world. For I was hungry and you gave me food, I was thirsty and you gave me drink, a stranger and you welcomed me, naked and you clothed me, ill and you cared for me, in prison and you visited me.' Then the righteous will answer him and say, 'Lord, when did we see you hungry and feed you, or thirsty and give you drink? When did we see you a stranger and welcome you, or naked and clothe you? When did we see you ill or in prison, and visit you?' And the king will say to them in reply, 'Amen, I say to you, whatever you did for one of these least brothers of mine, you did for me.' Then he will say to those on his left, 'Depart from me, you accursed, into the eternal fire prepared for the devil and his angels. For I was hungry and you gave me no food, I was thirsty and you gave me no drink, a stranger and you gave me no welcome, naked and you gave me no clothing, ill and in prison, and you did not care for me.' Then they will answer and say, 'Lord, when did we see you hungry or thirsty or a stranger or naked or ill or in prison, and not minister to your needs?' He will answer them, 'Amen, I say to you, what you did not do for one of these least ones, you did not do for me.' And these will go off to eternal punishment, but the righteous to eternal life."

» **Rather offensively, she calls God a 'Mother' in her writings...**

- "When times are most difficult, You are my Mother." (Diary, par. 239)

- "Jesus, I trust in You; I trust in the ocean of your mercy. You are a Mother to me." (Diary, par. 249)

- "Jesus, living Host, You are my Mother, You are my all! It is with simplicity and love, with faith and trust that I will always come to You, O Jesus! I will share everything with You, as a child with its loving mother, my joys and sorrows – in a word, everything." (Diary, par. 230)

- "You are always a most tender mother to me, and You surpass all mothers." (Diary, par. 1490)

What man - much less God - would be pleased to be called a mother, even if it is done with good intentions?

» Her diary gives the impression that God will have mercy on anyone who simply trusts in His mercy or appeals to His compassion...

- "All you souls, praise the Lord's mercy by trusting in His mercy all your life and especially at the hour of your death. And fear nothing[!], dear soul, whoever you are; the greater the sinner, the greater his right to Your mercy, O Lord" (Diary, par. 598)

- "He who trusts in My mercy will not perish, for all his affairs are mine, and his enemies will be shattered at the base of My footstool." (Diary, par. 723)

- "Every soul believing and trusting in My mercy will obtain it." (Diary, par. 420)

- "I cannot punish even the greatest sinner[!] if he makes an appeal to My compassion, but on the contrary, I justify him in My unfathomable and inscrutable mercy." (Diary, par. 1146)

- "When a soul approaches Me with trust, I fill it with such an abundance of graces that it cannot contain them within itself, but radiates them to other souls[!]." (Diary, par. 1074)

But this is problematic on a number of levels. For example...

1. Scripture speaks clearly of the need for repentance and the proper dispositions necessary to receive God's mercy (e.g. Lk. 1:50: "His mercy is from age to age to those who fear him."). Nowhere do I see trusting in His mercy mentioned in Holy Scripture.

2. Presumption is one of the six sins against the Holy Spirit. Yet her writings seems to dangerously lead souls down the road to presumption by insisting that sinners simply 'trust in His mercy', rather than emphasizing that they repent & amend their lives. As the Baltimore catechism teaches, "Presumption is a rash expectation of salvation without making proper use of the necessary means to obtain it" and warns that "The forgetfulness of God's justice will lead us into the sins of presumption." Clearly her writings may present a great danger of leading souls to presumption.

3. Unlike in Scripture where we told that...

"the wages of sin is death" (Rom. 6:23)

and that no sins or guilty persons go unpunished - e.g. "Do not plot to repeat a sin; not even for one will you go unpunished" (Sirach 7:8:) and "The Lord is slow to anger, yet great in power, and the Lord never leaves the guilty unpunished." (Nahum 1:3)

and where we are instructed to "fear God" (1 Pt. 2:17)

...she says Jesus "cannot punish even the greatest sinner if he makes an appeal to [His] compassion"!

» Her diary makes the novel claim that the greater the sinner, the greater right[!] he has to God's mercy ...

- "All you souls, praise the Lord's mercy by trusting in His mercy all your life and especially at the hour of your death. And fear nothing, dear soul, whoever you are; the greater the sinner, the greater his right to Your mercy, O Lord." (Diary, par. 598)

- "The greater the sinner, the greater his right to God's mercy" (Diary, par. 423)

- "The greater the sinner, the greater the right he has to My mercy." (Diary, par. 723)

- "Let the greatest sinners place their trust in My mercy. They have the right before others to trust in the abyss of My mercy." (Diary, par. 1146)

- "You are a bottomless sea of mercy for us sinners; and the greater the misery, the more right we have to Your mercy." (Diary, par. 793)

Since when we do we have a 'right' to a gift? And why does Scripture not speak of the sinner's 'right to mercy' (as if there was such a thing!), but rather speaks of punishment for sin? For example, consider these passages...

> Heb. 10:26-31: "If we sin deliberately after receiving knowledge of the truth, there no longer remains sacrifice for sins but a fearful prospect of judgment and a flaming fire that is going to consume the adversaries. Anyone who rejects the law of Moses is put to death without pity on the testimony of two or three witnesses. Do you not think that a much worse punishment is due the one who has contempt for the Son of God, considers unclean the covenant-blood by which he was consecrated, and insults the spirit of grace? We know the one who said:

'Vengeance is mine; I will repay,' and again: 'The Lord will judge his people.' It is a fearful thing to fall into the hands of the living God."

Rom.13:4: "But if you do evil, be afraid, for it does not bear the sword without purpose; it is the servant of God to inflict wrath on the evildoer."

Clearly, the greater the sinner, the greater right he has to judgment, NOT to mercy. He has a greater need of mercy, NOT a greater right to mercy.

» We also see other instances in her diary where justice is apparently thrown out the window...

- "Today the Lord said to me, My daughter, write down these words: All those souls who will glorify My mercy and spread its worship, encouraging others to trust in My mercy, will not experience terror at the hour of death. My mercy will shield them in that final battle..." (Diary, par. 1540)

- "Souls who spread the honor of My mercy I shield through their entire lives as a tender mother her infant, and at the hour of death I will not be a Judge for them [!], but the merciful Savior. At that last hour, a soul has nothing with which to defend itself except My mercy. Happy is the soul that during its lifetime immersed itself in the Fountain of Mercy, because justice will have no hold on it[!]." (Diary, par. 1075)

- "But God has promised a great grace especially to you and to all those...who will proclaim My great mercy. I shall protect them Myself at the hour of death, as My own glory." (Diary, par. 378)

But this contracts justice. One can spend one's time 'spreading the honor of God's mercy, glorifying, encouraging trust, and spreading worship' to God's mercy, and yet still be a great sinner. Yet we are to believe such sinners will fare well at

judgment? And what about the need for repentance? Again, this is omitted from her writings. Yet, how often the saints warned us to fear judgment! How often scripture tells us that God punishes sin! No propagation of any devotion will make up for failure to live up to God's requirements for salvation that are clearly laid out in Holy Scripture (e.g. performing good works, receiving the sacraments, following the commandments, etc.).

» Her diary makes reference to an image of Jesus that was painted (there was an original version and other versions followed later) that she says God "demands" be venerated. Her diary claims graces will flow to souls by means of this 'magical image' (my term). For example, her diary states...

- "By means of this Image I shall be granting many graces to souls; so, let every soul have access to it." (Diary, par. 570)

- "Then I heard these words: Not in the beauty of the color, nor of the brush lies the greatness of this image, but in My grace." (Diary, par. 313)

- "I demand the worship of My mercy through the solemn celebration of the Feast and through the veneration of the image which is painted. By means of this image I shall grant many graces to souls. It is to be a reminded of the demands of My mercy, because even the strongest faith is of no avail without works." (Diary, par. 742)

- "Today I saw the glory of God which flows from the image. Many souls are receiving graces, although they do not speak of it openly." (Diary, par. 1789)

- "I am offering people a vessel with which they are to keep coming for graces to the fountain of mercy. That vessel is this image with the signature: 'Jesus, I trust in You.'" (Diary, par. 327)

- "After a while, Jesus said to me, Paint an image according to the pattern you see, with the signature: Jesus, I trust in You. I desire that this image be venerated, first in your chapel, and [then] throughout the world. I promise that the soul that will venerate this image will not perish[!]. I also promise victory over [its] enemies already here on earth, especially at the hour of death. I Myself will defend it as My own glory." (Diary, par. 47-48)

Yet we know there can be NO new path to salvation and simply venerating an image will NOT save unrepentant sinners from hell! But, yet again, there is no call here to repentance.

Also, we know that God already instituted the sacraments to dispense His graces. He does not need to come back 1,900 years later to leave an image in order to dispense graces! Besides, sacraments give graces of themselves, whereas sacramentals do not give graces directly. [As stated in the Baltimore Catechism, "The difference between the Sacraments and the sacramentals is: 1st, The Sacraments were instituted by Jesus Christ and the sacramentals were instituted by the Church; 2nd, The Sacraments give grace of themselves when we place no obstacle in the way; the sacramentals excite in us pious dispositions, by means of which we may obtain grace."]

Furthermore, some think the image appears somewhat effeminate (I especially noticed this myself after a priest mentioned it to me). This is particularly noticeable in the original image.

Also, although some claim the original image matches 'exactly' with the Shroud of Turin, this is quite dubious. All one needs to do is compare the forehead and face shape on the original image to the Holy Shroud. There are clear differences in my opinion. Furthermore, if one was to cover the facial hair on the original image, it might be difficult to tell if the person represented was male or female. This is not so on the Shroud where one can clearly tell that the face on the image is masculine, even if one covers the facial hair.

The image also could be acceptable to Protestants as it is noticeably missing the Sacred Heart (some have therefore called the image 'heartless').

Furthermore, unlike many traditional images that Catholics may be used to, Faustina's Divine Mercy image has a dark (black) - and perhaps somewhat eerie - background.

Lastly, it is good to take note of the Baltimore Catechism's instruction concerning the possibility of sinning when using sacramentals: "Persons may sin in using Sacramentals by using them in a way or for a purpose prohibited by the Church; also by believing that the use of Sacramentals will save us in spite of our sinful lives. We must remember that Sacramentals can aid us only through the blessing the Church gives them and through the good dispositions they excite in us. They have, therefore, no power in themselves, and to put too much confidence in their use leads to superstition."

» She claims that no soul will be justified until it turns with confidence to God's mercy...

> "No soul will be justified until it turns with confidence
> to My mercy" (Diary, par. 570)

However, this contradicts Catholic theology in that, while we ARE required to have faith in God in order to be justified, we are NOT required specifically to 'turn in confidence to God's mercy' in order to be justified.

» She claims that the Feast of Mercy is "the last hope of salvation" - and she also claims that those who do not adore God's mercy will "perish for all eternity" (Diary, par. 965)! Yet the annual feast of mercy is unnecessary (Confession - the real 'last hope of salvation'! - is available every day, and even her version of the feast is essentially equivalent to a plenary indulgence - something that is also available every day). Furthermore, we cannot be required to adore God's mercy under penalty of hellfire based on a private revelation. This is an unheard of new 'mortal sin' and the Church CANNOT add to the deposit of faith that was passed on to the Apostles.

» Surprisingly, her diary claims that Jesus is 'wounded' more by lack of trust and 'disbelief' than He is by actual sin (even though sin is "the greatest evil in the world" according to the Catechism of St. John Neumann)...

- "My child, all your sins have not wounded My Heart as painfully as your present lack of trust does" (Diary, par. 1486)

- "Tell her that her disbelief wounds My heart more than the sins she committed" (Diary, par. 628)

» Her diary also seems question the need for Purgatory (see http://www.mycatholicsource.com/mcs/tp/topic_page-purgatory.htm), at least for certain persons (she does not deny that there is a Purgatory). For example, consider this passage...

"I often attend upon the dying and through entreaties obtain for them trust in God's mercy, and I implore God for an abundance of divine grace, which is always victorious. God's mercy sometimes touches the sinner at the last moment in a wondrous and mysterious way. Outwardly, it seems as if everything were lost, but it is not so. The soul, illumined by a ray of God's powerful final grace, turns to God in the last moment with such a power of love that, in an instant, it receives from God forgiveness of sin and punishment [!], while outwardly it shows no sign either of repentance or of contrition, because souls [at that stage] no longer react to external things." (Diary, par. 1698)

Assuming here for argument's sake that the soul she references did repent internally (i.e. had perfect contrition) and thereby actually did receive forgiveness without Confession, that certainly does not remit the punishment that is due. As indicated in Holy Scripture, no sin goes unpunished (Sirach 7:8: "Do not plot to repeat a sin; not even for one will you go unpunished").

Also, it would seem much better for Faustina to focus on praying for the necessary grace of repentance than on praying for the person to attain "trust in God's mercy".

» All in all, Faustina's diary seems to present a rather dangerous message that God is so anxious to be merciful and so reluctant to punish - whereas Scripture says differently (e.g. Sirach 5:7: "mercy and anger alike are with Him").

As probably most parents with children over a certain age know, an overemphasis on mercy may very well result in bad behavior as there are apparently no negative consequences to be had. In the long-run, sometimes true love means not showing mercy - sometimes showing mercy isn't merciful at all! For example, consider the case of a drug addict. Showing mercy may actually help such a person continue in his addiction, rather than encourage him to change his ways. Likewise, few people may be motivated to do something difficult for their boss, judge, or other superior if this person constantly emphasized how merciful they are and likewise told of their reluctance to punish.

Who will really be motivated to amend their lives by an overemphasis on God's mercy? We see in Scripture, that Jesus wasn't a 'pushover', nor did He place a very strong emphasis on God's mercy. Rather, Jesus preached repentance (Mt. 4:17: "From that time on, Jesus began to preach and say, 'Repent, for the kingdom of heaven is at hand'"). The need for repentance and the threat of Hell are far more likely to prompt people to amend their ways than talking about God's mercy!

Even though Faustina assures us over and over again that the message of mercy 'snatches souls from hell', doesn't common sense tell us that an overemphasis on mercy is much more likely to lead souls towards hell than snatch souls from hell? While sinners may like to hear of God's mercy, how will this cause them to amend their ways? Especially when the message in her diary doesn't at all emphasize the need to amend one's life, but rather seeks to have sinners simply 'trust in His mercy'.

+++

Errors & theological problems in Faustina's writings are especially troubling, given that she claims to have such a special knowledge of God (see above for examples). In her diary, she also claims that...

> "There are moments when God introduces the soul to a purely spiritual state. The senses dim and are seemingly dead. The soul is most closely united to God; it is immersed in the Deity; its knowledge is complete and perfect, not sporadic as before, but total and absolute." (Diary, par. 115)

Given this claim, aren't theological errors in her writings even more unacceptable? Certainly errors wouldn't come from God!

+++

And this brings me to my next point, namely that Faustina wasn't always certain of her own experiences. For example, consider the following passages in her diary...

- "In the evening during benediction, such thoughts as these began to distress me: Is not perhaps all this that I am saying about God's great mercy just a lie or an illusion..." (Diary, par. 359)

- "Once again, a terrible darkness envelops my soul. It seems to me that I am falling prey to illusions." (Diary, par. 211)

- "People have often sown doubt in my soul, and I myself have sometimes become frightened at the thought that I was, after all, an ignorant person and did not have knowledge of many things, above all, spiritual things" (Diary, par. 121)

- "But I distrusted myself so much that I made up my mind to put an end to the doubts once and for all. I therefore looked forward with special eagerness to the retreat before perpetual vows. But even for many days before the retreat, I kept on asking God to give light to the priest who would hear my confession, so that he could say, once and for all, either yes or no. And I thought to myself, 'I'll be set at peace once and for all.'" (Diary, par. 213)

- "At first I agreed, but the next day I decided I would not go to Mother Directress, because I was not sure whether this had happened in a dream or in reality. And so I did not go." (Diary, par. 21) *[Isn't it concerning that Faustina has difficulty knowing whether something happened in a dream or in reality?]*

- "I have wasted many of God's graces because I was always afraid of being deluded." (Diary, par. 143)

- "My only desire was that some priest would say this one word to me, 'Be at peace, you are on the right road,' or 'Reject all this for it does not come from God.' But I could not find such a priest who was sufficiently sure of himself to give me a definite opinion in the name of the Lord. And so the uncertainty continued." (Diary, par. 127)

- "I began to avoid encounters with the Lord in my soul because I did not want to fall prey to illusions." (Diary, par. 130)

And despite all the alleged heavenly illuminations she claims she received, she also says she needs clarifications from other people ...

> "I often feel that, apart from Jesus, I get no help from anyone, although sometimes I am very much in need of clarifications concerning the demands of the Lord." (Diary, par. 744)

She furthermore admits one can "easily" fall prey to illusions...

> "There is a series of graces which God pours into the soul after these trials by fire. The soul enjoys intimate union with God. It has many visions, both corporeal and intellectual. It hears many supernatural words, and sometimes distinct orders. But despite these graces, it is not self-sufficient. In fact, it is even less so as a result of God's graces, because it is now open to many dangers and can easily fall prey to illusions." (Diary, par. 121)

And at one point, she even admits that her 'visions' were purely interior...

> "My visions are purely interior" (Diary, par. 883)

Various other persons that knew her were also not confident in her experiences. For example, consider these passages from her diary...

- "Once during Holy Mass, I felt in a very special way the closeness of God, although I tried to turn away and escape from Him. On several occasions I have run away from God because I did not want to be a victim of the evil spirit; since others have told me, more than once, that such is the case" (Diary, par. 40)

- "There was one thing which I could not understand for a long time: Jesus ordered me to tell everything to my Superiors, but

94

my Superiors did not believe what I said and treated me with pity as though I were being deluded or were imagining things." (Diary, par. 38)

- "she is the first of the superiors who did not cause me any doubts in this regard" (Diary, par. 222)

- "What I said to you was said as a warning, because illusions may afflict even holy persons, and Satan's insinuations may play a part in this, and sometimes this comes from our own selves, so one has to be careful." (Diary, par. 646)

- "He said to me, 'I cannot discern what power is at work in you, Sister, perhaps it is God and perhaps it is the evil spirit.'" (Diary, par. 211)

- "Oh, how much I feel I am in exile! I see that no one understands my interior life." (Diary, par. 1141)

- "I see that even the superiors do not always understand the road along which God is leading me, and I am not surprised at this." (Diary, par. 761)

- "For quite a long time I was regarded as one possessed by the evil spirit, and I was looked upon with pity, and the superior took certain precautionary actions in my respect. It reached my ears that the sisters also regarded me as such. And the sky grew dark around me. I began to shun these divine graces, but it was beyond my power to do so. Suddenly, I would be enveloped in such recollection that, against my will, I was immersed in God, and the Lord kept me completely dependent upon Himself." (Diary, par. 123)

- "When I opened up my soul still more deeply, I did not obtain what I desired; it seemed to my superior that these graces [of which I was the object] were unlikely, and so I could not draw any further help from her. She told me it was impossible that God should commune with His creatures in such a way: 'I fear for you, Sister; isn't this an illusion of some sort! You'd better go, Sister, and talk about these matters with your superiors.' And so I would go from the superiors to the confessor and from the confessor to the superiors, and I found no peace. These divine graces became a great suffering for me. And more than once I said to the Lord directly, 'Jesus, I am afraid of You; could You not be some kind of a ghost?'" (Diary, par. 122)

- "When some inner force urged me again not to put off this matter, I was unable to find peace. I told the confessor, Father Bukowski, that I could not wait any longer. Father answered me, 'Sister, this is an illusion. The Lord Jesus cannot be demanding this. You have made your perpetual vows. All this is an illusion. You are inventing some sort of heresy!' And he was shouting at me, almost at the top of his voice. I asked him whether all of this was an illusion, and He said, 'Everything.' 'Then please tell me what course I must take.' 'Well, Sister, you must not follow any inspiration. You should get your mind off all this. You should pay no attention to what you hear in your soul and try to carry out your exterior duties well. Give no thought to these things and put them completely out of your mind.'" (Diary, par. 643)

- "Today, I had a conversation with Father [Andrasz] and he recommended great caution in the matter of these sudden appearances of the Lord Jesus. When he was speaking about divine mercy, some sort of strength and power entered my heart. My God, I want so much to express everything and am so very unable to do so. Father tells me that the Lord Jesus is very generous in communicating himself to souls and, on the other hand, He is, so to speak, stingy. 'Although God's generosity is very great,' said Father, 'be careful anyway, because these sudden appearances arouse suspicion; although, personally, I do not see anything wrong here, or anything contrary to faith.* Be a little more careful, and when Mother Superior comes, you can talk to her about these things.'" (Diary, par. 1068) *[* Note: He may not have examined everything, and he spoke to her only 'personally'.]*

As a result of problems she encountered, Faustina stopped telling of her experiences to her superiors...

"When I saw that my mind was not being set at rest by my superiors, I decided to say nothing [to them] of these purely interior matters. Exteriorly I tried, as a good nun should, to tell everything to my superiors, but as for the needs of my soul, I spoke about these only in the confessional." (Diary, par. 123)

We also see that when others did finally believe her experiences, she apparently just disregarded all the others who did not believe in them as being wrong. We also see that those who agree with her experiences tend to be singled out for praise (even supposedly by God), while those who do not trust in them may be criticized. For example, consider this passage...

"Once, when I saw that God had tried a certain Archbishop [Jalbrzykowski] because he was opposed to the cause and distrustful of it, I felt sorry for him and pleaded with God for him, and God relieved his suffering. God is very displeased with lack of trust in Him, and this is why some souls lose many graces." (Diary, par. 595)

Notice how she equates the Archbishop's being distrustful of "the cause" with a lack of trust in God! Is the Archbishop not to use the mind God gave Him? Is this really a lack of trust in Him (God) or her (Faustina)? I think the answer is clear.

Overall, she tends to regard those who distrust her experiences as 'inexperienced', not understanding, on Satan's side, etc. She seems to give very little acknowledgement to the fact that her amazing & extraordinary claims would be hard for many sane, knowledgeable Catholics to believe simply on her own say so.

Furthermore, she doesn't seem to have any clue that her writings may be problematic from a doctrinal point of view.

$$+++$$

Although some of these doctrinal matters were covered above, briefly it is useful to elaborate a bit more on a few points, namely her diary's apparent overemphasis on and omissions concerning God's mercy.

Yes, it is true that God is merciful...

- "His mercy endures forever" - Dan. 3:89 (et al.)

- "All your ways are mercy and truth" - Tobit 3:2

- "But you have mercy on all, because you can do all things; and you overlook the sins of men that they may repent" - Wisdom 11:23

- "For equal to his majesty is the mercy that he shows." - Sirach 2:18

- "Let your spirits rejoice in the mercy of God, and be not ashamed to give him praise." - Sirach 51:29

- "Hear, O Lord, for you are a God of mercy" - Baruch 3:2

- "God, who is rich in mercy" - Eph. 2:4

- "So let us confidently approach the throne of grace to receive mercy and to find grace for timely help." - Heb. 4:16

But it is likewise true that NOT all persons will receive mercy - and those who do NOT receive mercy, do NOT fail to receive mercy simply because they lack trust. Scripture says the following about those who will receive or who will not receive

mercy (note that NONE of the reasons people receive or don't receive mercy depends on trust)...

- "I who grant mercy to whom I will." - Ex. 33:19

- "His mercy is from age to age to those who fear him." - Lk. 1:50

- "Blessed are the merciful, for they will be shown mercy." - Mt. 5:7

- "...but bestowing mercy, down to the thousandth generation, on the children of those who love me and keep my commandments" - Deut. 5:10

- "He who conceals his sins prospers not, but he who confesses and forsakes them obtains mercy." - Prov. 28:13

- "How great the mercy of the Lord, his forgiveness of those who return to him!" - Sirach 17:24

- "Those who worship vain idols forsake their source of mercy." - Jonah 2:9

- "Of forgiveness be not overconfident, adding sin upon sin. Say not: 'Great is his mercy; my many sins he will forgive.' For mercy and anger alike are with him; upon the wicked alights his wrath. Delay not your conversion to the Lord, put it not off from day to day; For suddenly his wrath flames forth; at the time of vengeance, you will be destroyed." - Sirach 5:5-9

- "And had there been but one stiffnecked man, it were a wonder had he gone unpunished. For mercy and anger alike are with him who remits and forgives, though on the wicked alights his wrath." - Sirach 16:11

- "Great as his mercy is his punishment; he judges men, each according to his deeds." - Sirach 16:12

- "And you have done worse than your fathers. Here you are, every one of you, walking in the hardness of his evil heart instead of listening to me. I will cast you out of this land into a land that neither you nor your fathers have known; there you can serve strange gods day and night, because I will not grant you my mercy." - Jer. 16:12-13

- "Therefore, as I live, says the Lord God, because you have defiled my sanctuary with all your detestable abominations, I swear to cut you down. I will not look upon you with pity nor have mercy." - Ezek. 5:11

- "Now the end is upon you; I will unleash my anger against you and judge you according to your conduct and lay upon you the consequences of all your abominations. I will not look upon you with pity nor have mercy; I will bring your conduct down upon you, and the consequences of your abominations shall be in your midst; then shall you know that I am the Lord." - Ezek. 7:3-4

- "Soon now I will pour out my fury upon you and spend my anger upon you; I will judge you according to your conduct and lay upon you the consequences of all your abominations. I will not look upon you with pity nor have mercy; I will deal with you according to your conduct, and the consequences of your abominations shall be in your midst; then shall you know that it is I, the Lord, who strike." - Ezek. 7:8-9

- "Consequently, he has mercy upon whom he wills, and he hardens whom he wills. You will say to me then, 'Why (then) does he still find fault? For who can oppose his will?' But who indeed are you, a human being, to talk back to God? Will what is made say to its maker, 'Why have you created me so?' Or does not the potter have a right over the clay, to make out of the same lump one vessel for a noble purpose and another for an ignoble one? What if God, wishing to show his wrath and make known his power, has endured with much patience the vessels of wrath made for destruction? This was to make known the riches of his glory to the vessels of mercy, which he has prepared previously for glory, namely, us whom he has called, not only from the Jews but also from the Gentiles." - Rom. 9:18-24

- "So speak and so act as people who will be judged by the law of freedom. For the judgment is merciless to one who has not shown mercy; mercy triumphs over judgment." - Jms. 2:12-13

Furthermore, Faustina's message of God being so anxious to dispense His mercy - apparently without repentance - is surely NOT the same message that is in Holy Scripture - it is certainly NOT the message that Jesus gave when he walked the earth. Scripture speaks clearly about God's mercy, but it is very balanced and necessitates the proper dispositions necessary to receive it. Her diary greatly overemphasizes mercy and practically ignores the need for repentance. Even a simple word count clearly bears this out. For example, we see ...

In the New Testament... (NAB Translation)

- Mercy/merciful is mentioned 40 + 7 = 47 times

- Repent* is mentioned 51 times

In all of Holy Scripture... (NAB Translation)

- Mercy/merciful is mentioned 190 + 42 = 232 times

- Repent* is mentioned 82 times

In Faustina's Diary... (all inclusive)

- Mercy/merciful is mentioned 1,335 + 142 = 1,477 times

- Repent* is mentioned 17 times

In her diary, mercy/merciful is mentioned MANY MORE times than it is in ALL of New Testament put together, whereas repent/repentance is mentioned in her diary FAR LESS than it is in Holy Scripture.

To be more exact...

- Her diary mentions mercy/merciful 31 times for every one single time it is mentioned in the New Testament (her diary mentions mercy/merciful 1,477 times whereas the entire New Testament mentions mercy/merciful just 47 times)

- Her diary mentions mercy/merciful 6 times for every single time it is mentioned in the entire Bible (her diary mentions mercy/merciful 1,477 times whereas the entire Bible mentions mercy/merciful just 232 times)

- Her diary mentions repent/repentance only 17 times, yet repent/repentance is mentioned 51 times in the New Testament

- Her diary mentions mercy more than 86 times for every one time repent/repentance is mentioned (mercy/merciful is mentioned a total of 1,477 times, whereas repent/repentance is mentioned just 17 times total)

- In the New Testament, repent/repentance is mentioned 4 times MORE than mercy/merciful is mentioned (51 times vs. 47 times), yet her diary reverses this and mentions mercy/merciful 1460 times more than it mentions repent/repentance (1,477 times vs. 17 times)

Clearly her diary contains a LARGE OVEREMPHASIS on mercy and an BIG UNDER-EMPHASIS of the need to repent in order to obtain mercy. Additionally, even when considering the few mentions of repent/repentance that appear in her diary, it

should be noted that almost none of these mentions are used in the context of calling persons to repentance. To illustrate, the following are the seventeen (17) passages in her diary that refer to repent/repentance - that is, these are the ONLY passages in her ENTIRE diary that mention repent/repentance...

[Please note: To make this point more clear, items below may be partial paragraphs where just the relevant word is contained, and the word repent/repentance is emphasized (in bold).]

1. "O sweet Jesus, it is here You established the throne of Your mercy To bring joy and hope to sinful man, From Your open Heart, as from a pure fount, Flows comfort to a **repentant** heart and soul." (Diary, par. 1)

2. "On one occasion I saw two sisters who were about to enter hell. A terrible agony tore my soul; I prayed to God for them, and Jesus said to me, Go to Mother Superior and tell her that those two sisters are in danger of committing a mortal sin. The next day I told this to the Superior. One of them had already **repented** with great fervor and the other was going through a great struggle." (Diary, par. 43)

3. "Once the Lord said to me, My Heart was moved by great mercy towards you, My dearest child, when I saw you torn to shreds because of the great pain you suffered in **repenting** for your sins." (Diary, par. 282)

4. "See what grace and reflection made out of the greatest criminal. He who is dying has much love: 'Remember me when You are in paradise.' Heartfelt **repentance** immediately transforms the soul. The spiritual life is to be lived earnestly and sincerely." (Diary, par. 388)

5. "Rejoice, all you creatures, for you are closer to God in His infinite mercy than a baby to its mother's heart. O

God, You are compassion itself for the greatest sinners who sincerely **repent**." (Diary, par. 423)

6. "All night long, I was preparing to receive Holy Communion, since I could not sleep because of physical suffering. My soul was flooded with love and **repentance**." (Diary, par. 717)

7. "The **repentance** of my heart is linked to love." (Diary, par. 852)

8. "O Jesus, how sorry I feel for poor sinners. Jesus, grant them contrition and **repentance**." (Diary, par. 908)

9. "Small practices for Lent. Although I wish and desire to do so, I cannot practice big mortifications as before, because I am under the strict surveillance of the doctor. But I can practice little things: first – sleep without a pillow; keep myself a little hungry; every day, with my arms outstretched, say the chaplet ...occasionally, with arms outstretched, for an indefinite period of time, pray informally. Intention: to beg divine mercy for poor sinners, and for priests, the power to bring sinful hearts to **repentance**." (Diary, par. 934)

10. "O my Jesus, I beg You on behalf of the whole Church: Grant it love and the light of Your Spirit, and give power to the words of priests so that hardened hearts might be brought to **repentance** and return to You, O Lord." (Diary, par. 1052)

11. "Today I wore a chain belt for seven hours in order to obtain the grace of **repentance** for that soul." (Diary, par. 1248)

12. "Especially in the tribunal of Your mercy does my soul meet an ocean of favors, though You did not give the Fallen Angels time to **repent**" (Diary, par. 1489)

13. "Tell My priests that hardened sinners will **repent** on hearing their words" (Diary, par. 1521)

14. "... while outwardly it shows no sign either of **repentance** or of contrition" (Diary, par. 1698)

15. "I called convents into being to sanctify the world through them. It is from them that a powerful flame of love and sacrifice should burst forth. And if they do not **repent** and become enkindled by their first love, I will deliver them over to the fate of this world" (Diary, par. 1702)

16. "I cannot love a soul which is stained with sin; but when it **repents**, there is no limit to My generosity toward it." (Diary, par. 1728)

17. "During this reading, my soul was filled with deep **repentance**." (Diary, par. 1766)

The above represents EVERY SINGLE INSTANCE in her entire diary where repent/repentance is mentioned. These few occasions where repent/repentance appear in her diary are greatly overshadowed by frequent mention of the terms mercy/merciful. Her diary is hardly a call to repentance! Nor do such few mentions of repentance really emphasize any real need for repentance in order to obtain mercy (read the passages above and see for yourself). Furthermore, these few mentions of repentance in her diary get practically lost in the 200,000+ word treatise of hers. This is in clear & stark contrast to the New Testament in which we see the need for repentance being central/essential. For example, we find these passages in the New Testament...

- "In those days John the Baptist appeared, preaching in the desert of Judea and saying, 'Repent, for the kingdom of heaven is at hand!'" - Mt. 3:1-2

- "From that time on, Jesus began to preach and say, "Repent, for the kingdom of heaven is at hand." - Mt. 4:17

- "John (the) Baptist appeared in the desert proclaiming a baptism of repentance for the forgiveness of sins." - Mk. 1:4

- "After John had been arrested, Jesus came to Galilee proclaiming the gospel of God: 'This is the time of fulfillment. The kingdom of God is at hand. Repent, and believe in the gospel.'" - Mk 1:14-15

- "He summoned the Twelve and began to send them out two by two and gave them authority over unclean spirits... So they went off and preached repentance." - Mk. 6:7, 6:12

- "In the fifteenth year of the reign of Tiberius Caesar, when Pontius Pilate was governor of Judea, and Herod was tetrarch of Galilee, and his brother Philip tetrarch of the region of Ituraea and Trachonitis, and Lysanias was tetrarch of Abilene, during the high priesthood of Annas and Caiaphas, the word of God came to John the son of Zechariah in the desert. He went throughout the whole region of the Jordan, proclaiming a baptism of repentance for the forgiveness of sins" - Lk. 3:1-3

- "He said to them in reply, 'Do you think that because these Galileans suffered in this way they were greater sinners than all other Galileans? By no means! But I tell you, if you do not repent, you will all perish as they did! Or those eighteen people who were killed when the tower at Siloam fell on them - do you think they were more guilty than everyone else who lived in Jerusalem? By no means! But I tell you, if you do not repent, you will all perish as they did!'" - Lk. 13:2-5

- "I tell you, in just the same way there will be more joy in heaven over one sinner who repents than over ninety-nine righteous people who have no need of repentance." - Lk.15:7

- "In just the same way, I tell you, there will be rejoicing among the angels of God over one sinner who repents." - Lk.15:10

- "And he said to them, 'Thus it is written that the Messiah would suffer and rise from the dead on the third day and that repentance, for the forgiveness of sins, would be preached in his name to all the nations, beginning from Jerusalem.'" - Lk. 24:46-47

- "Now I know, brothers, that you acted out of ignorance, just as your leaders did; but God has thus brought to fulfillment what he had announced beforehand through the mouth of all the prophets, that his Messiah would suffer. Repent, therefore, and be converted, that your sins may be wiped away" - Acts 3:17-19

- "John heralded his coming by proclaiming a baptism of repentance to all the people of Israel" - Acts 13:24

- "God has overlooked the times of ignorance, but now he demands that all people everywhere repent" - Acts 17:30

- "And so, King Agrippa, I was not disobedient to the heavenly vision. On the contrary, first to those in Damascus and in Jerusalem and throughout the whole country of Judea, and then to the Gentiles, I preached the need to repent and turn to God, and to do works giving evidence of repentance." - Acts 26:19-20

- "The present heavens and earth have been reserved by the same word for fire, kept for the day of judgment and of destruction of the godless. But do not ignore this one fact, beloved, that with the Lord one day is like a thousand years and a thousand years like one day. The Lord does not delay his promise, as some regard 'delay,' but he is patient with you, not wishing that any should perish but that all should come to repentance." - 2 Pt. 3:7-9

As a final proof that repentance is not central or emphasized in Faustina's writings, note that a word count of her diary shows that the following words (among many others) are mentioned more often than repent/repentance are mentioned...

- joy (mentioned 223 times)

- interior (mentioned 179 times)

- suddenly (mentioned 142 times)

- profound* (mentioned 74 times)

- omnipoten* (mentioned 52 times)

- ground* (mentioned 38+ times)

- cloth* (mentioned 26+ times)

- thirst* (mentioned 23 times)

- tired* (mentioned 22 times)

Even the word 'crystal' is mentioned 16 times (just one shy of the number of times repent/repentance is mentioned - namely, 17 times).

Besides the lack of mention regarding the need for repentance to obtain mercy, her diary also seems to focus on mercy at expense of fear of the Lord. Her diary explicitly tells sinners (apparently even non-repentant sinners) NOT to be afraid...

- "Let the sinner not be afraid to approach Me." (Diary, par. 50) *[Notice that this doesn't say 'repentant sinner']*

- "Let the weak, sinful souls have no fear to approach Me" (Diary, par. 1059) *[Again, this doesn't say 'repentant sinful souls']*

- "Let no soul fear to draw near to Me, even though its sins be as scarlet." (Diary, par. 699) *[Again, no talk about repenting]*

- "Tell sinful souls not to be afraid to approach Me" (Diary, par. 1396) *[Still no talk about repentance]*

Yet we know that Holy Scripture: (1) tells us to fear God, (2) is critical of those who don't fear the Lord (for example, see Ps. 55:20, Rom. 3:13-18), (3) praises fear of the Lord, and (4) even tells us to work out our salvation "with fear and trembling" (see Phil. 2:12). Below are some sample passages from Holy Scripture...

- "The last word, when all is heard: Fear God and keep his commandments, for this is man's all" - Eccl. 12:13

- "With all your soul, fear God, revere his priests." - Sirach 7:29

- "Whose offspring can be in honor? Those of men. Which offspring are in honor? Those who fear God. Whose offspring can be in disgrace? Those of men. Which offspring are in disgrace? Those who transgress the commandments." - Sirach 10:19

- "Give honor to all, love the community, fear God, honor the king." - 1 Pt. 2:17

- "He said in a loud voice, 'Fear God and give him glory, for his time has come to sit in judgment. Worship him who made heaven and earth and sea and springs of water.'" - Rv. 14:7

- "The fear of God is a paradise of blessings; its canopy, all that is glorious." - Sirach 40:27

- "The fear of the Lord is the beginning of wisdom; prudent are all who live by it." - Ps. 111:10

- "The fear of the Lord is the beginning of knowledge; wisdom and instruction fools despise." - Prov. 1:7

- "The beginning of wisdom is the fear of the Lord, and knowledge of the Holy One is understanding." - Prov. 9:10

- "The fear of the Lord is a fountain of life, that a man may avoid the snares of death." - Prov. 14:27

- "The fear of the Lord is training for wisdom, and humility goes before honors." - Prov. 15:33

- "Fear of the Lord is glory and splendor, gladness and a festive crown." - Sirach 1:9

- "The beginning of wisdom is fear of the Lord, which is formed with the faithful in the womb." - Sirach 1:12

- "Fullness of wisdom is fear of the Lord; she inebriates men with her fruits." - Sirach 1:14

- "The root of wisdom is fear of the Lord; her branches are length of days." - Sirach 1:18

- "Wealth and vigor build up confidence, but better than either, fear of God. Fear of the Lord leaves nothing wanting; he who has it need seek no other support" - Sirach 40:26

- "Fear of the Lord surpasses all else. its possessor is beyond compare." - Sirach 25:11

- "Unless you earnestly hold fast to the fear of the Lord, suddenly your house will be thrown down." - Sirach 27:3

There is no talk here about the sinner simply 'trusting in God's mercy'. Rather, Scripture warns sinners in no uncertain terms that "it is a fearful thing" to "fall into the hands of the living God"...

"If we sin deliberately after receiving knowledge of the truth, there no longer remains sacrifice for sins but a fearful prospect of judgment and a flaming fire that is going to consume the adversaries. Anyone who rejects the law of Moses is put to death without pity on the testimony of two or three witnesses. Do you not think that a much worse punishment is due the one who has contempt for the Son of God, considers unclean the covenant-blood by which he was consecrated, and insults the spirit of grace? We know the one who said: 'Vengeance is mine; I will repay,' and again: 'The Lord will judge his people.' It is a fearful thing to fall into the hands of the living God." - Heb. 10:26-31

Any who might point to 1 John 4:18 regarding there being 'no fear in love' ["There is no fear in love, but perfect love drives out fear because fear has to do with punishment, and so one who fears is not yet perfect in love"], should take heed of the footnote to this passage in the Douay Rheims bible...

"Perfect charity, or love, banisheth human fear, that is, the fear of men; as also all perplexing fear, which makes men mistrust or despair of God's mercy; and that kind of servile fear, which makes them fear the punishment of sin more than the offence offered to God. But it no way excludes the wholesome fear of God's judgments, so often recommended in holy writ; nor that fear and trembling, with which we are told to work out our salvation."

Clearly sinners who are sincerely repentant should not have fear to approach God to make amends for their deeds, but this is not the message that her diary gives. As indicated above, her diary practically excludes the entire notion of repentance altogether and exchanges it for a simple 'trust in God's mercy'.

While it is true that God's mercy is great, her writings may (dangerously) bring people to think & act as if God has no wrath against - or that He would not exercise judgment on - those who simply 'trust in Him'. In her diary, there is almost no talk about repentance, contrition, an intention to amend one's life, making restitution, etc., even though these are all necessary for forgiveness. She paints an image of God that seems to contradict passages like these in Holy Scripture...

- "A jealous and avenging God is the Lord, an avenger is the Lord, and angry; The Lord brings vengeance on his adversaries, and lays up wrath for his enemies" - Nahum 1:2

- "Of forgiveness be not overconfident, adding sin upon sin. Say not: 'Great is his mercy; my many sins he will forgive.' For mercy and anger alike are with him; upon the wicked alights his wrath. Delay not your conversion to the Lord, put it not off from day to day; For suddenly his wrath flames forth; at the time of vengeance, you will be destroyed." - Sirach 5:5-9

- "God is a just judge, who rebukes in anger every day." - Ps. 7:12

Compare the above Scripture passages with the Jesus of her diary who supposedly says: "My hand is reluctant to take hold of the sword of justice." (Diary, par. 1588)

Her writings also give the impression that for some people there may be no repaying for or consequences for sins. Yet scripture says...

- "Do not plot to repeat a sin; not even for one will you go unpunished." - Sirach 7:8

- "Make no mistake: God is not mocked, for a person will reap only what he sows" - Gal. 6:7

- "Behold, I am coming soon. I bring with me the recompense I will give to each according to his deeds." - Rv. 22:12

- "I saw the dead, the great and the lowly, standing before the throne, and scrolls were opened. Then another scroll was opened, the book of life. The dead were judged according to their deeds, by what was written in the scrolls. The sea gave up its dead; then Death and Hades gave up their dead. All the dead were judged according to their deeds." - Rv. 20:12-13

- "Amen, amen, I say to you, the hour is coming and is now here when the dead will hear the voice of the Son of God, and those who hear will live. For just as the Father has life in himself, so also he gave to his Son the possession of life in himself. And he gave him power to exercise judgment, because he is the Son of Man. Do not be amazed at this, because the hour is coming in which all who are in the tombs will hear his voice and will come out, those who have done good deeds to the resurrection of life, but those who have done wicked deeds to the resurrection of condemnation. I cannot do anything on my own; I judge as I hear, and my judgment is just, because I do not seek my own will but the will of the one who sent me." - Jn. 5:25-30

- "When the Son of Man comes in his glory, and all the angels with him, he will sit upon his glorious throne, and all the nations will be assembled before him. And he will separate them one from another, as a shepherd separates the sheep from the goats. He will place the sheep on his right and the goats on his left. Then the king will say to those on his right, 'Come, you who are blessed by my Father. Inherit the kingdom prepared for you from the foundation of the world.

For I was hungry and you gave me food, I was thirsty and you gave me drink, a stranger and you welcomed me, naked and you clothed me, ill and you cared for me, in prison and you visited me.' Then the righteous will answer him and say, 'Lord, when did we see you hungry and feed you, or thirsty and give you drink? When did we see you a stranger and welcome you, or naked and clothe you? When did we see you ill or in prison, and visit you?' And the king will say to them in reply, 'Amen, I say to you, whatever you did for one of these least brothers of mine, you did for me.' Then he will say to those on his left, 'Depart from me, you accursed, into the eternal fire prepared for the devil and his angels. For I was hungry and you gave me no food, I was thirsty and you gave me no drink, a stranger and you gave me no welcome, naked and you gave me no clothing, ill and in prison, and you did not care for me.' Then they will answer and say, 'Lord, when did we see you hungry or thirsty or a stranger or naked or ill or in prison, and not minister to your needs?' He will answer them, 'Amen, I say to you, what you did not do for one of these least ones, you did not do for me.' And these will go off to eternal punishment, but the righteous to eternal life." - Mt. 25:31-46

We see clearly in Holy Scripture that Jesus is a just judge - one who judges deeds - and that no sin will go unpunished. Yet she paints a picture of a very merciful (rather than just) judge who is always ready to dispense mercy to whoever trusts in Him (apparently without even the need for contrition or repentance) and one who is reluctant to exercise justice or punish sin. Clearly, this is NOT the same picture that we see in Holy Scripture!

Also, Faustina repeatedly - and erroneously - refers to God's mercy as His 'greatest attribute' (she even states that mercy "surpasses[!] all His other qualities" - see Diary, par. 611). For example, consider the following passages from her diary...

114

- "Oh, how great is the mercy of the Lord; it surpasses all His other qualities! Mercy is the greatest attribute of God" (Diary, par. 611)

- "Proclaim that mercy is the greatest attribute of God." (Diary, par. 301)

- "The mercy of the Lord I will sing forever, Before all the people will I sing it, For it is God's greatest attribute And for us an unending miracle." (Diary, par. 522)

- "Let Your mercy resound throughout the orb of the earth, and let is rise to the foot of Your throne, giving praise to the greatest of Your attributes; that is, Your incomprehensible mercy." (Diary, par. 835)

- "... how ardently I desire to glorify this greatest of Your attributes; namely, Your unfathomable mercy." (Diary, par. 835)

- "Eternal Father, turn Your merciful gaze upon the souls who glorify and venerate Your greatest attribute, that of Your fathomless mercy" (Diary, par. 1225)

- "It will be the reflection of God's greatest attribute; that is, His divine mercy." (Diary, par. 664)

Yet, mercy cannot really be God's 'greatest attribute'. If mercy is God's 'greatest attribute', this would mean His other attributes (e.g. goodness, wisdom, love, etc.) are not as great - which is clearly absurd! Also, if mercy was truly God's greatest attribute, that would mean the He does not have equal perfections - which is clearly wrong as God is perfect in all respects. Also, we must ask...

- If mercy is God's "greatest attribute", why does scripture say "mercy and anger alike are with Him" (see Sirach 5:7, 16:11)

- If mercy is God's "greatest attribute", why had the Church not taught this - or even heard of this - for 1,900 years? Why did Jesus not teach this when he walked the earth? Why did no one know this for the thousands of years of human history? Why didn't God mention it before? And why did He put mercy on par with anger if mercy is "greatest"?

- If mercy is God's "greatest attribute", why is it sinful to presume it? If mercy is His "greatest attribute", why should we not expect it?

- Considering that God never needed to make a creature (He only chose to create us out of His goodness), and that without creatures God would never have an opportunity to exercise mercy, how can mercy be considered God's "greatest attribute"?

- If mercy is God's "greatest attribute", why is it Faustina claimed He wanted to set up a congregation to beg for His mercy? We don't have to beg for His other attributes (e.g. love or goodness)

- If mercy is God's "greatest attribute", why is it sometimes denied? His other attributes are never denied or withheld (e.g. goodness, wisdom)

- If mercy is God's "greatest attribute", how is it that we - His insignificant creatures by comparison - can stop Him from giving mercy to us? We can't stop His love or His goodness, but we can stop His mercy, so how can mercy be the "greatest" attribute?

- Unlike other attributes of God (e.g. wisdom, love, goodness), His mercy may be partially dependent on OUR actions (e.g. asking for mercy). So how can mercy therefore be His greatest attribute?

- If mercy is God's "greatest attribute", why was it 'dormant' from all eternity until after creatures were made, after the fall? His other attributes (e.g. wisdom, love, goodness), weren't dormant from all eternity

- If mercy is God's "greatest attribute", why was it denied to His first creatures (the angels - namely those angels who fell)?

- If mercy is God's "greatest attribute", why is there a hell? If the answer is justice, than how can mercy be the "greatest attribute" if justice can win out over mercy? Doesn't that mean justice is greater than mercy? If you answer that the condemned "chose" their lot, then you are saying human beings' choice is effectively greater than God's "greatest attribute"?!

- How is it that mercy is supposed to be God's "greatest attribute", but what we need mercy for is to save us from His punishments?

- If mercy is God's "greatest attribute" how is it that Faustina could claim Jesus doesn't want purgatory but His justice "demands" it? If mercy was His "greatest attribute" wouldn't mercy win out?

- If mercy is God's "greatest attribute", why are few saved rather than many? [Mt. 22:14: "Many are invited, but few are chosen.", And: Mt. 7:13-14: "Enter through the narrow gate; for the gate is wide and the road broad that leads to destruction, and those who enter through it are many. How narrow the gate and constricted the road that leads to life. And those who find it are few." And: Lk. 13:23-24: "Someone asked (Jesus), 'Lord, will only a few people be saved?' He answered them, 'Strive to enter through the narrow gate, for many, I tell you, will attempt to enter but will not be strong enough.'"] Don't answer that they chose to be damned because we see in Scripture that persons are damned who apparently didn't want to be damned (see above).

Are we really supposed to believe that Jesus - who is perfect in every regard - picked out a single attribute of His - one that He wouldn't ever even use if not for us creatures - as His GREATEST? That He is therefore saying His other attributes are LESS great? Seriously? While no one is denying that God's mercy is very great, it seems very doctrinally unsound to claim that mercy is His "greatest" attribute. Also, keep in mind that it is one thing for an individual to have an opinion that mercy is God's "greatest attribute", whereas it's quite another thing to believe that Jesus said mercy is His "greatest" attribute!

I cannot emphasize enough how critical this concept of mercy being God's "greatest attribute" is to Faustina's message and devotion. If mercy is not God's "greatest attribute", her writings concerning God's mercy would seem to unravel as the message seems to be 'built' on this assertion (that is supposedly uttered by and emphasized by Christ). Yet, this assertion cannot possibly be true. So what does that say about her devotion and her writings?

But, as is clear from above, this is not the only point of her writings that appears doctrinally unsound. Another especially troubling aspect of her writings is the idea that those who simply "trust" in God's mercy will receive it. Surprisingly, she makes very little mention of people going to Confession to receive mercy* -- yet this is precisely where Jesus himself established that God's mercy would be dispensed. It is the priest who has the power to bestow God's mercy, as Scripture indicates...

[* Note: She does mention that the tribunal of mercy is Confession, but: (1) it is not at all emphasized, and (2) this reference doesn't appear until paragraph 1448, close to 2/3 of the way through her entire 200,000+ word diary.]

"And when he had said this, he breathed on them and said to them, 'Receive the Holy Spirit. Whose sins you forgive are forgiven them, and whose sins you retain are retained.'" - Jn. 20:22-23 *[Note here that priests have the power to both forgive AND retain sins. Priests cannot always dispense forgiveness/mercy in the confessional.]*

Also, this power of dispensing mercy was granted ONLY to the Apostles (and to their lawful successors & to priests). Yet Sister Faustina claims she herself has the power to dispense God's mercy (outside the confessional). In her diary, she claims Jesus told her...

- "You, who are the dispenser of My mercy, tell all the world about My goodness, and thus you will comfort My Heart." (Diary, par. 580)

- "Relieve My deathly sorrow; dispense My mercy." (Diary, par. 975)

- "My daughter, I desire that your heart be an abiding place of My mercy. I desire that this mercy flow out upon the whole world through your [!] heart." (Diary, par. 1777)

She also claims she has the power to dispense graces...

"I heard these words, Do whatever you wish, distribute graces as you will, to whom you will and when you will." (Diary, par. 31)

And she says that Jesus wants people to adore His mercy - or else they will be condemned...

"If they will not adore My mercy, they will perish for all eternity." (Diary, par. 965)

Which begs the questions: If we must adore God's mercy to be saved, why is this not mentioned in Holy Scripture? Why was this not taught from Apostolic times? Why do we not have to

likewise adore His just anger since Scripture says "mercy and anger alike are with him" (Sirach 5:7)? And, curiously, why is it that Faustina's 'message of mercy' threatens damnation for a brand new 'mortal sin' that was never before heard of? Is this merciful?

Some additional thoughts concerning her theology with reference to trusting / adoring God's mercy...

- Scripture says Jesus "will come with his angels in his Father's glory, and then he will repay everyone according to his conduct" (Mt. 16:27), not according to whether or not they worshipped His mercy or trusted in it

- It is very possible to simultaneously be very trusting in Jesus' mercy and also be in a state of mortal sin. Yet, it is of faith that a person who died in this state would go to Hell, not heaven - despite the great trust!

- Scripture tells us over and over again that we will be judged according to deeds, yet Faustina's devotion puts forth the idea that we will be judged according to whether or not we had trust in or worshipped His mercy - now He will render not according to works, but according to our 'trust'? How many passages of scripture does this contradict!

- Scripture tells us that "If you keep my commandments, you will remain in my love" (Jn. 15:10). Scripture does NOT say "if you trust in my mercy you will remain in my love"!

- How is it that the whole message of scripture seems to be directing us to live in accordance with God's laws - not worshipping His mercy - something which isn't even mentioned by Jesus - yet we are to believe our salvation now depends on worshiping His mercy?

- Why does Jesus tell us in Scripture to prepare for His coming by being watchful if what we are really supposed to be doing is trusting in His mercy?

- How can it be that simply trusting/worshipping mercy will be enough when Scripture says "Do not be deceived; neither fornicators nor idolaters nor adulterers nor boy prostitutes nor practicing homosexuals nor thieves nor the greedy nor drunkards nor slanderers nor robbers will inherit the kingdom of God." (1 Cor. 6:9-10)?

- How can her version of Jesus place an such emphasis on adoring mercy/trusting in mercy when scripture tells us that "Religion that is pure and undefiled before God and the Father is this: to care for orphans and widows in their affliction and to keep oneself unstained by the world" (Jms. 1:27)? If adoring His mercy was so important, why didn't it even rate a mention?

- If people need to adore God's mercy to be saved, isn't this a rather large thing to be left out of Scripture - and out of all of the Church's history & tradition? Why is talk of adoring God's mercy or trusting it entirely omitted from Holy Scripture if it is so important and necessary?

- How can it be a sin to NOT trust in His mercy? If 'not trusting' in His mercy is a mortal sin, why is it the that Church always taught the opposite - that is, against presumption? The Church has always promoted a proper balance between despair and presumption, but Faustina's devotion very heavily tends towards presumption

- If this emphasis on 'trusting' in God's mercy is true, why does Scripture tell us Christ is the source of salvation "for all who obey him" (Heb. 5:9), rather than for all those who trust in Him & worship His mercy?

121

- Given the clear teaching of Scripture and the constant teaching of the Church regarding judgment, how can people seriously believe they will stand before the tribunal of Christ and receive their sentence according to their 'trust' in God's mercy rather than according to their actual deeds?

- How is it that Scripture speaks of "the elect" as being the ones who are saved - and that these people are NOT put forth merely as being persons who "trusted in God's mercy"?

- How is it possible that followers of this devotion are to believe that they will be saved if they adore/trust in God's mercy while they disobey God? Scripture says "whoever disobeys the Son will not see life, but the wrath of God remains upon him" (Jn. 3:36) - no matter how trusting they may be in God's mercy!

- How does a sinner's adoring God's mercy and trusting in it make him worthy to stand before God when nothing unclean can enter heaven? ("but nothing unclean will enter it, nor any one who does abominable things or tells lies." - Rv. 21:27)

- If failing to worship/trust in God's mercy results in damnation, why does Scripture paint a different picture of those who will be left out (e.g. "But as for cowards, the unfaithful, the depraved, murderers, the unchaste, sorcerers, idol-worshipers, and deceivers of every sort, their lot is in the burning pool of fire and sulfur, which is the second death." - Rv. 21:8)?

- Why do we see much in the Apocalypse/Revelation about "fury and wrath" - rather than calls to trust in God's mercy? Especially how is this so considering that this devotion is supposed to be a preparation for Christ's second coming?

- Scripture could not be more clear about what judgment is based on - and it is NOT trust in or adoration of God's mercy (e.g. "I bring with me the recompense I will give to each according to his deeds" - Rv. 22:12), so why do Faustina's writings base judgment on adoration of & trust in God's mercy?

Clearly there are points of her writings that attempt to impose new doctrine (e.g. see below), but Catholics are called to reject such items. New doctrinal additions to the faith are NOT acceptable! The Church has always taught this, and Scripture also instructs us...

- "But even if we or an angel from heaven should preach (to you) a gospel other than the one that we preached to you, let that one be accursed! As we have said before, and now I say again, if anyone preaches to you a gospel other than the one that you received, let that one be accursed!" - Gal. 1:8-9

- "See to it that no one captivate you with an empty, seductive philosophy according to human tradition, according to the elemental powers of the world and not according to Christ." - Col. 2:8

- "Jesus Christ is the same yesterday, today, and forever. Do not be carried away by all kinds of strange teaching." - Heb. 13:8-9

- "Anyone who is so 'progressive' as not to remain in the teaching of the Christ does not have God; whoever remains in the teaching has the Father and the Son. If anyone comes to you and does not bring this doctrine, do not receive him in your house or even greet him; for whoever greets him shares in his evil works." - 2 Jn. 1:9-11

- "I charge you in the presence of God and of Christ Jesus, who will judge the living and the dead, and by his appearing and his kingly power: proclaim the word; be persistent whether it is convenient or inconvenient; convince, reprimand, encourage through all patience and teaching. For the time will come when people will not tolerate sound doctrine but, following their own desires and insatiable curiosity, will accumulate teachers and will stop listening to the truth and will be diverted to myths. But you, be self-possessed in all circumstances; put up with hardship; perform the work of an evangelist; fulfill your ministry." - 2 Tm. 4:1-5

+ + +

Furthermore, it is clear that Faustina's version of Jesus seems so different from the real Jesus (see http://www.mycatholicsource.com/mcs/tp/topic_page-Jesus.htm) that we see in Holy Scripture, both in terms of His speech and His actions. For example, who can picture the Jesus of Holy Scripture (or in some cases, any man) speaking in the way Faustina claims Jesus spoke in her diary...

- "Tell your confessor that I commune with your soul in such an intimate manner because you do not steal My gifts" (Diary, par. 1069)

- "Your sincere love is as pleasing to My Heart as the fragrance of a rosebud at morningtide, before the sun has taken the dew from it. The freshness of your heart captivates Me; that is why I united Myself with you more closely than with any other creature" (Diary, par. 1546)

- "Do you think that I will not have enough omnipotence to support you?" (Diary, par. 527)

- "Tell aching mankind to snuggle close to My merciful Heart" (Diary, par. 1074)

- "I am the Lord in My essence and am immune to orders or needs." (Diary, par. 85)

- "I understand you because I am God-Man." (Diary, par. 797)

- "Know, My daughter, that the simpler your speech is, the more you attract Me to yourself." (Diary, par. 797)

- "Jesus stood by my side and said. My daughter, what are you thinking about right now?" (Diary, par. 960)

- "I saw the Lord Jesus leaning over me, and He asked, My daughter, what are you writing?" (Diary, par. 1693)

- "This evening, the Lord asked me, Do you not have any desires in your heart?" (Diary, par. 1700)

- "That evening Jesus said to me, I want you to stay home." (Diary, par. 64)

- "I am concerned about every beat of your heart. Every stirring of your love is reflected in My Heart. I thirst for your love." (Diary, par. 1542)

- "My daughter, I assure you of a permanent income on which you will live. Your duty will be to trust completely in My goodness, and My duty will be to give you all you need." (Diary, par. 548)

- "Know that you are now on a great stage where all heaven and earth are watching you." (Diary, par. 1760)

- Etc. [Note: See below for more examples]

Or who can picture the Jesus of Holy Scripture being the 'hugger' that he is portrayed as being in Faustina's diary...

- "I saw the Lord, who clasped to me to His Heart" (Diary, par. 928)

- "Jesus pressed me to His Heart" (Diary, par. 853)

- "During Holy Mass, I saw the Lord, who said to me, Lean your head on My breast and rest. The Lord pressed me to His Heart..." (Diary, par. 1053)

- "Today, the Lord visited me, pressed me to His Heart and said, Rest, My little child, I am always with you." (Diary, par. 1011)

- Etc. [Note: See below for more examples]

Likewise, the Blessed Virgin Mary (see http://www.mycatholicsource.com/mcs/tp/topic_page-Blessed_Virgin_Mary.htm) seems quite different in Faustina's diary than we know her to be from Holy Scripture (e.g. hugging, wearing transparent clothing, handing off Jesus and disappearing, etc.) (see below)

+ + +

Faustina's accounts also seem to contradict - or at least not be on the same page as - Marian apparitions at Fatima (see http://www.mycatholicsource.com/mcs/tp/topic_page-fatima.htm) which occurred near the same time that Faustina wrote (1917 and later , vs. 1930's). For example, consider these differences between the Fatima apparitions and Faustina's writings...

- Fatima gives a very Catholic 'heavenly peace plan' that involves stopping sin, praying the Rosary daily, doing the consecration, wearing the scapular, performing penance/acts of reparation, etc. In contrast, Faustina writes...

  "Tell aching mankind to snuggle close to My merciful Heart, and I will fill it with peace." (Diary, par. 1074)

  "Mankind will not have peace until it turns with trust to My mercy." (Diary, par. 300)

"Mankind will not have peace until it turns to the Fount of My Mercy." (Diary, par. 699)

- Fatima emphasizes repentance & penance, whereas Faustina emphasizes mercy

- At Fatima, a great sign was given to prove the apparition's authenticity, whereas Faustina's apparitions were not accompanied by a great sign

- Unlike the message at Fatima that didn't contradict itself and contained prophecies which came true, Faustina's writings contain contradictions (see below) & prophecies that did not come true (see below)

- At Fatima, the Blessed Virgin Mary urged us to pray the Holy Rosary, whereas Faustina urges that we use rosary beads to instead pray a chaplet that she dictates (rather than using the beads to pray the Rosary)

- At Fatima, there is a warning of chastisement due to sin, whereas Faustina's writings seem to let sinners off the hook (e.g. by simply having them 'trust in God's mercy'), without even emphasizing that sinners need to change their ways

- At Fatima, there is a call to devotion to the Immaculate Heart of Mary, whereas Faustina focuses on adoring & trusting in God's mercy. Rather than emphasizing devotion to the Blessed Virgin Mary, Faustina's writings typically show that Mary was there to comfort & assist Faustina

- At Fatima, we are encouraged to amend our ways and make reparation, whereas Faustina's writings encourage us to 'trust in God's mercy' and venerate an image (neither of which lead a person to holiness)

- Mary called for a consecration of Russia at Fatima, yet Faustina never mentions this fact even though the consecration had not been done. (I believe Our Lady first mentioned the consecration she would later request on July 13, 1917, and she asked for the consecration on June 13, 1929, whereas Faustina's writings were in made the 1930's.) So if the Blessed Virgin was appearing to her as well, why was there no mention of this consecration in her diary?

- Bl. Jacinta of Fatima said that "The Blessed Mother can no longer restrain the hand of her Divine Son from striking the world with just punishment for its many crimes", yet Faustina's focus is not on repentance or stopping sin, but rather 'trusting God's mercy'

Overall both apparitions have a very different focus and a very different message. Fatima is distinctly Catholic and ties in well with tradition & Holy Scripture. Faustina's writings, on the other hand, sometime appear to favor Protestant ideas (try here for 'Those Outside the Church' Topic Page: http://www.mycatholicsource.com/mcs/tp/topic_page-those_outside_the_Church.htm). For example, consider these points of affinity between Faustina's Divine Mercy devotion & Protestantism...

- Her writings seems to put forth another type of 'saved by faith alone' doctrine (e.g. with its emphasis on belief in/trusting in God's mercy for salvation - perhaps Faustina's could be called a 'trust alone' doctrine)

- Her writings promise mercy for those who believe ('trust'), rather for than those who repent and act rightly

- Her writings tend to de-emphasize the importance of the sacraments for attaining mercy

- Her writings tend to de-emphasize the power of the priest for obtaining mercy

- Her writings tend to substitute the need for amending one's life with a mere faith (or rather, a mere 'trust' in mercy)

- Her writings give the idea that there are shortcuts to salvation (e.g. 'trusting in God's mercy')

- She puts forth an image which can be used by Protestants (it is 'heartless', as it does not contain the Sacred Heart of Jesus - a traditional Catholic image which may offend Protestants)

- She promotes 'priest-less deaths' (her devotion urges praying the chaplet for the dying, but doesn't suggest calling a priest)

- Her writings help foster a Protestant mentality [e.g. presumption of mercy / no fear of judgment for those who believe ('trust')]

- Etc.

+++

Faustina's writings also have much to please modernists - "the worst enemies of the Church" according to Bl. Pope Pius IX. *[Note: For more on modernism, try here: http://www.mycatholicsource.com/mcs/tp/topic_page-modernism.htm.]* **For example...**

- **Barren churches**: "There were no decorations and no kneelers in the chapel." (Diary, par. 613) *[Note: See http://www.mycatholicsource.com/mcs/qt/church_talk_reflect ions.htm for 'Church Talk' Reflections]*

- **Lack of vestments**: "Today, I saw how the Holy Mysteries were being celebrated without liturgical vestments and in private homes, because of a passing storm" (Diary, par. 991) *[Note: See http://www.mycatholicsource.com/mcs/qt/priests_and_vocati ons_reflections.htm for Priests & Vocations Reflections]*

- **Egalitarian**: "There will be no distinction between the sisters, no mothers, no reverends, no venerables, but all will be equal" (Diary, par. 538)

- **Lay dress**: "The persons living in this convent were still wearing lay clothes, but a thoroughly religious spirit reigned there, and I was organizing everything just as the Lord wanted." (Diary, par. 1154) And "There will never be any splendid houses, but only a small church with a small community consisting of a few souls, not more than ten, plus two externs to look after the external affairs of the community and the church. These two sisters will not wear the habit, but secular dress; they will take simple vows, and they will depend strictly on the superior who will be cloistered." (Diary, par. 536) *[Note: See http://www.mycatholicsource.com/mcs/qt/church_talk_reflect ions.htm for 'Church Talk' Reflections]*

- **Head uncovered/women in sanctuary**: "Then I saw the Mother of God in a white garment and blue mantle, with Her head uncovered [!]. She approached me from the altar [!], touched me with Her hands and covered me with Her mantle, saying, Offer these vows for Poland. Pray for her." (Diary, par. 468) And "I [Faustina] quickly took my place [!] on the altar." (Diary, par. 31) *[Note: See http://www.mycatholicsource.com/mcs/tp/topic_page-catholic_women.htm for Catholic Women Topic Page]*

- **Laity handling holy objects**: "When I re-entered my cell, I saw the ciborium with the Blessed Sacrament, and I heard this voice, Take this ciborium and bring it to the tabernacle. I hesitated at first, but when I approached and touched it, I heard these words, Approach each of the sisters with the same love with which you approach Me; and whatever you do for them, you do it for Me. A moment later, I saw that I was alone." (Diary, par. 285) And: "I went in spirit to the Tabernacle and uncovered the ciborium, leaning my head on the rim of the cup, and all my tears flowed silently toward the

Heart of Him who alone understands what pain and suffering is." (Diary, par. 1454) And: "A hand placed the ciborium in front of me, and I took it in my hands" (Diary, par. 640) *[Note: See http://www.mycatholicsource.com/mcs/pc/sacraments/lay_mi nisters__why_not.htm for "Lay 'Eucharistic Ministers': Why Not?"]*

- **Laity handling the Holy Eucharist**: "And the Host came out of the tabernacle and came to rest in my hands and I, with joy [not fear!], placed it back in the tabernacle. This was repeated a second time, and I did the same thing. Despite this, it happened a third time, but the Host was transformed into the living Lord Jesus, who said to me, I will stay here no longer! At this, a powerful love for Jesus rose up in my soul, I answered, "And I, I will not let You leave this house, Jesus!" [!] And again Jesus disappeared while the Host remained in my hands. [!] Once again I put it back in the chalice and closed it up in the tabernacle. And Jesus stayed with us. I undertook to make three days of adoration by way of reparation." (Diary, par. 44) *[Note: See http://www.mycatholicsource.com/mcs/pc/sacraments/commu nion_in_the_hand__why_not.htm for 'Communion in the Hand: Why Not?']*

- **Communion in the hand**: "This was my day for keeping watch before the Lord Jesus. It was my duty to make amends to the Lord for all offenses and acts of disrespect and to pray that, on this day, no sacrilege be committed. This day, my spirit was set aflame with special love for the Eucharist. It seemed to me that I was transformed into a blazing fire. When I was about to receive Holy Communion, a second Host fell onto the priest's sleeve, and I did not know which host I was to receive. After I had hesitated for a moment, the priest made an impatient gesture with his hand to tell me I should receive the host. When I took the Host he gave me, the other one fell onto my hands. The priest went along the altar rail to distribute Communion, and I held the Lord Jesus in my hands all that time. When the priest approached me again, I raised the Host for him to put it back into the chalice, because when I had first received Jesus I could not speak before consuming the Host, and so could not tell him that the other had fallen. But while I was holding the Host in my hand, I felt such a power of love that for the rest of the day I could neither eat nor come to my senses. I heard these words from the Host: I desired to rest in your hands, not only in your heart. And at that moment I saw the little Jesus. But when the priest approached, I saw once again only the Host." (Diary, par. 160) - And keep in mind that this was before the disobedience of Communion in the hand was tolerated! *[Note: See http://www.mycatholicsource.com/mcs/pc/sacraments/communion_in_the_hand__why_not.htm for 'Communion in the Hand: Why Not?']*

- **God's presence in general vs. Christ's presence in the Holy Eucharist**: "During Holy Mass, I again saw the little Infant Jesus, extremely beautiful, joyfully stretching out His little arms to me. After Holy Communion, I heard the words: I am always in your heart; not only when you receive Me in Holy Communion, but always." (Diary, par. 575) *[Note: See http://www.mycatholicsource.com/mcs/qt/sacraments_reflections_Holy_Eucharist_Mass__Real_Presence.htm for Reflections on the Real Presence]*

- **Woman to instruct priests (contrary to scripture)**: "My daughter, speak to priests about this inconceivable mercy of Mine." (Diary, par. 177) *[Note: See http://www.mycatholicsource.com/mcs/pc/vocations/top_reasons_why_women_cant_be_priests.htm for 'Top Reasons Why Women Can't Be Priests']*

- **Laity/women sent forth to teach (based on Faustina's erroneous vision of the Ascension)**: "Today I accompanied the Lord Jesus as He ascended into heaven. It was about noon. I was overcome by a great longing for God. It is a strange thing, the more I felt God's presence, the more ardently I desired Him. Then I saw myself in the midst of a huge crowd of disciples and apostles, together with the Mother of God. Jesus was telling them.... Go out into the whole world and teach in My name." (Diary, par. 1710) *[Note: Besides the fact that women teaching contradicts Holy Scripture (see above), her vision is also in error on another level. Namely, the Gospel account of the Ascension in Mark 16:14-20 does NOT indicate that there was "a huge crowd of disciples and apostles, together with the Mother of God" who were sent to teach. Rather, it states that Jesus commissioned the eleven (ALL male) apostles: "But later, as the eleven [!] were at table, he appeared to them and rebuked them for their unbelief and hardness of heart because they had not believed those who saw him after he had been raised. He said to them, 'Go into the whole world and proclaim the gospel to every creature. Whoever believes and is baptized will be saved; whoever does not believe will be condemned. These signs will accompany those who believe: in my name they will drive out demons, they will speak new languages. They will pick up serpents (with their hands), and if they drink any deadly thing, it will not harm them. They will lay hands on the sick, and they will recover.' So then the Lord Jesus, after he spoke to them, was taken up into heaven and took his seat at the right hand of God. But they went forth and preached everywhere, while the Lord worked with them and confirmed the word through accompanying signs."] (Note: See http://www.mycatholicsource.com/mcs/qt/priests_and_vocati ons_reflections_priesthood.htm for Reflections on Priests / The Priesthood)*

+ + +

Her writings also risk doing damage / producing bad fruit - possibly even leading to the loss of souls! For example devotees of this devotion...

- may lack necessary repentance

133

- may not be motivated to amend their lives

- may be guilty of the sin of presumption

- may omit sacraments

- may neglect other devotions and therefore lose benefits to be
  had from those true devotions

- may fail to receive the last sacraments at death (as they may
  not see the importance of the sacraments relative to
  Faustina's claims regarding the chaplet) - possibly to the loss
  of their souls

- may be encouraged to spend their time promoting this
  devotion (in order to receive the supposed benefit of faring
  well at judgment) instead of working on their personal
  holiness - something that actually may have helped them to
  fare well at judgment

- may be subject to special difficulties at death (for example,
  devotees may agonize at death because they simultaneously
  feel they are supposed to trust in God's mercy (presume their
  salvation), yet Catholic teaching urges them to have
  reasonable fear regarding judgment. Persons who have the
  proper disposition regarding judgment may simultaneously
  feel they are failing to 'trust in God's mercy - it could be a
  vicious cycle)

The devotion may also...

- sow confusion / errors

- cast doubt on Catholic doctrine (e.g. need for confession)

- Protestantize the Catholic mindset among both priests & laity

- suit the interests of Satan more than God (e.g. due to presumption, lack of repentance)

- encourage people to believe in new revelations & new doctrines which can't be true

- fail to promote holiness

- make people not concerned about judgment / cause people to deceive themselves about not being judged (remember what her writings claim about those who promote the devotion and about those who venerate the image)

- overshadow true & worthy Catholic devotions (e.g. Rosary, Sacred Heart) *[Note: For more information on the Holy Rosary, try here: http://www.mycatholicsource.com/mcs/tp/topic_page-holy_rosary.htm. For more information on the Sacred Heart of Jesus, try here: http://www.mycatholicsource.com/mcs/tp/topic_page-Sacred_Heart.htm]*

- overshadow (and apparently contradict) true & worthy apparitions and their messages (e.g. Fatima) (see above)

- cause sacraments not to be dispensed when they should be - even at death!

- lead to sin (because there is no fear)

- promote an improper mindset at the most critical hour of one's life (death) *[Note: For more on death, try here: http://www.mycatholicsource.com/mcs/tp/topic_page-death.htm]*

- distract persons away from the greatest celebration of all - Easter *[Note: For more on Easter, try here:*

http://www.mycatholicsource.com/mcs/tp/topic_page-easter.htm]

- cause persons to fail to do what should be done at death (get a priest vs. say a chaplet) - and this could cost souls!

- make Catholics look bad to those outside the Church and possibly hinder others' conversions (how can the Church promote an apparition with contradictions & prophecies that didn't come true?)

- scandalize Catholics (how can the Church promote an apparition with doctrinal issues, contradictions & prophecies that didn't come true?)

What other devotion risks such damage? Besides, Faustina's Divine Mercy devotion can seem so cultish, complete with shirts, bumper stickers, etc. for those supposedly 'enlightened' Catholics who are 'in love with' the message. Unfortunately, such persons may wholeheartedly hold fast to the devotion - come what may - because they 'feel' it is true, rather than because they have looked at the facts & applied critical thinking skills. It seems impossible to make headway with people who prefer to think with their feelings instead of with the head that God gave them.

And, should someone point to alleged good fruits from the devotion, I am reminded of Medjugorje [see http://www.mycatholicsource.com/mcs/pc/the_Blessed_Virgin/m edjugorje_true_or_false.htm], which also claims supposed 'good fruits'. Even if there were some good fruits associated with this devotion, this can't compensate for the bad ones. Nor can supposed good fruits make a false devotion true. Furthermore, if people eventually come to realize their beloved devotion is false, they may lose their faith altogether.

+ + +

Remember that NO NEW DOCTRINE can be added to the deposit of faith and that private revelations absolutely CANNOT BE REQUIRED for salvation - so it is TOTALLY SAFE to ignore this devotion.

And, considering that there is no real, indisputable proof for this devotion's authenticity, ignoring it should be even easier. Remember that...

- Even though the Church may approve a devotion, it cannot with absolute certainly guarantee that the devotion is true and comes from God, nor can the Church impose the devotion or require belief in it

- The assertions come from her diary and her alleged mystical experiences have no real, verifiable corroboration to speak of

- Her writings contains many errors (see below), contradictions (see below), and false prophecies that did not materialize (see below), whereas true apparitions should be free of doctrinal errors and false prophecies

- Her writings contain a number of elements that are theologically problematic (e.g. see above)

- Faustina herself received spiritual counsel that "If these inspirations are not in accord with the faith or the spirit of the Church, they must be rejected immediately as coming from the evil spirit." (Diary, par. 55)

- Unlike the apparitions at Fatima just a few years previous, Faustina's much more elaborate apparitions were NOT confirmed with a great sign (like the apparitions at Fatima were - i.e. the miracle of the sun)

- There is a lack of visible proof concerning what Faustina claims - and others can't testify to seeing what she claims to have seen since so much of what she reports occurred internally. Furthermore, Faustina had her own doubts about what she saw (see above)

- We know for a fact that Faustina can be deceived about what she saw (she admittedly burned her own diary after being deceived by a supposed angel who 'later turned out to be Satan' - and this even though she was supposedly under St. Michael's special protection!)

- This devotion was originally prohibited by the Church - at a time when the Church had unquestionably sound judgment (as opposed to more recent times when scandalous ecumenical activities have occurred, when a pope has kissed the Koran, when a pope has apologized so frequently for the Church's past, etc.)

- This 'happy' devotion conveniently fits in well with the Novus Ordo Mass of the 1960's (see: http://www.mycatholicsource.com/mcs/tp/topic_page-novus_ordo_mass.htm) which removed negative topics from scripture readings. And it also fits in well with the Vatican II novelty of using a "medicine of mercy" (and we see how poorly this 'medicine of mercy' has worked for decades now in the declining Church statistics!)

- Everything concerning this devotion is essentially based on Faustina's own written testimony - with no cross examination possible

- Even concerning supposed proofs (e.g. special knowledge regarding dying persons), we know that this information could have been imparted by an evil spirit (who has much to gain by people presuming in God's mercy instead of repenting)

- Faustina's message contains so many phenomenal claims - for her, 'the miraculous is commonplace' - that it sets a very high bar for credibility, yet offers no real proof

- Curiously, her message of mercy threatens damnation for a new 'mortal sin' that was never before heard of (namely failing to adore God's mercy). Imagine, threatening people that they must worship God's mercy under penalty of eternal ruin!

- Also curiously & quite problematically, her message of mercy seems to practically short circuit the known & God-given means of mercy (e.g. perfect contrition, and in particular, the need for the sacrament of Penance).

So how is it possible that this devotion got Church approval? One thing is for sure, a fellow Pole (Pope John Paul II) liked the devotion and took it upon himself to get approval for the devotion and also obtained canonization of the Polish nun, Sister Faustina (previously the devotion was forbidden).

Normally it would be encouraging that something was promoted by a pope, but in this happens to be the same pope who kissed the Koran, gave away a Catholic icon, issued apologies for the Church's past, engaged in scandalous ecumenical activities, approved a scandalous ecumenical directory, failed to resolve problems with abusive priests, etc. *[Try here for related user article: http://www.mycatholicsource.com/mcs/ua/user_article-when_a_pope_should_be_called_great.htm.]* **So, we are unfortunately not able to be so sure with respect to his approval of this devotion - especially since it is not a matter where infallibility is involved.** *[For more on infallibility, see: http://www.mycatholicsource.com/mcs/pc/vatican_view/papal_infalli bility.htm.]*

Another possible reason the devotion received approval is that it tends to prop up Vatican II with its 'medicine of mercy'. *[For more on Vatican II, try here: http://www.mycatholicsource.com/mcs/tp/topic_page-second_vatican_council.htm.]* **Likewise, various persons in the Church wanting Faustina's ('pleasing-to-the-ears') message to be true certainty didn't hurt! Perhaps the message was so liked that**

some particulars concerning her writings were 'overlooked' or excused away & rationalized.

Yet even despite the Church's approval, we must remember that...

- Approval of the diary/devotion is NOT infallible

- Approval of the diary/devotion does NOT guarantee that it is genuine

- Canonization of Faustina does NOT guarantee that her experiences were genuine or that her 'doctrines' are true

- The devotion CANNOT be imposed on us

- We are NOT required to believe in the devotion

- It is a very bad time in the Church today - a lot of things which have gone on in the Church's recent past are wrong, despite Church approval or being carried on by a prelate (e.g. scandalous sex ed programs, Communion in the hand, scandalous ecumenical activities, etc.)

- It is unlikely that this devotion would been approved before Vatican II (again, it was previously forbidden). In fact, it is unlikely that this devotion would have been approved - or that the (Polish) Sister Faustina would have been canonized - under any other pope that the (also Polish) Pope John Paul II. Even staunch devotees of this devotion may freely admit these facts.

Yes, her diary may be captivating - complete with tales of heavenly beings, special graces, and a great heroine who seems to passionately love God & suffering - and it may be the "in" devotion in the Church today, but as good Catholics we must care about truth. Yes, God is very merciful, but that fact alone doesn't make Faustina's Divine Mercy devotion true. As

indicated above, Faustina apparently does love God much, suffer much, and say many humble things. She also had no financial aim and no apparent malicious intent. Yet that doesn't prevent her from being unintentionally and sincerely misled (or even deceived by the prince of lies). One only has to look at the many errors, contradictions and false prophecies - not to mention astonishing claims and uncharacteristic portrayals of Jesus & Mary - in her writings to know that something is wrong.

Catholics must not put aside critical thinking skills. We are told in Holy Scripture to reject false teachings and we are also told in Holy Scripture that prophecies that don't come true were not from God. We must also remember that this devotion has great potential for harm (see above) and that the devil has much to gain by it (e.g. if people presume God's mercy instead of repenting). Faustina's Divine Mercy message is NOT the same message of repentance that is portrayed in Holy Scripture. Yes, God is merciful, but He doesn't say in Scripture that He wants us to worship and trust in His mercy. Rather, He tells us He wants us to stop sinning, repent, and utilize the sacraments so that we may receive His mercy!

+ + +

In closing, I will leave with some questions to be pondered...

- How can this devotion be true - particularly the threat of a new 'mortal sin' - considering that it is new doctrine, yet the idea of new doctrine has been condemned by the Church? (see above)

- How can a devotion promoting mercy bring with it the threat of a new & previously unheard of 'mortal sin'?

- How can her writings be true since they contain contradictions? (see below)

141

- How can her writings be true since they contain prophecies that never came true? (see below)

- How can the author's credibility be entirely assured given that she admitted to lying/misrepresenting herself in the past? (see above)

- How can we believe that Jesus was so amazingly doting on Faustina considering that He was never known to be so doting to the real Apostles or to other saints, or even to His Blessed Mother?

- How is it that a devotion focused on mercy does not contain a call to frequent Confession? Why is it not really a call to Confession at all? (Yes, there is some mention, but this is severely overshadowed by all the mercy talk - Confession is definitely NOT given much emphasis)

- Why is it that the Church teaches us that forgiveness is based on repentance whereas Faustina gives the overall impression that mercy is given based on trust in mercy? Why is repentance from sin noticeably missing from most of her diary?

- Why does the known Jesus emphasize avoiding sin, conversion & penance whereas Faustina's version of Jesus emphasizes trusting in mercy without much call to avoiding sin, conversion or penance?

- Why do these alleged apparitions contain so much emphasis on the person of Sister Faustina - unlike other known apparitions (e.g. Fatima, Lourdes, etc.)?

- How can we trust the theology of a nun who consented to the baptizing of an adult Jewish woman without her permission? Especially how can we trust the nun's theology considering that she rejoiced that this un-converted Jewish woman supposedly entered heaven despite the fact that she rejected

142

Jesus and despite the fact that Jesus says faith is required for salvation? (see above)

- Why does Faustina so frequently mention suffering & trials, which doesn't seem very characteristic for saints? (e.g. see above)

- We see that Faustina constantly claims that Jesus came to reassure her - What other saint has received such attention? And why have others NOT received such attention?

- Why does Faustina's version of Jesus seem to be so talkative during Mass?

- How is it possible Faustina could have remembered conversations with Jesus, superiors, etc. in such amazing detail, right down to the words used? Especially since she was so frequently suffering? She writes paragraphs supposedly quoting Jesus and others (e.g. spiritual director), yet how many persons could remember in such amazing detail if they were not even taking notes?

- Why do Faustina's writings claim that Jesus is taking such special care of her - like no one else ever before? How is this possible considering the many holy men and women who have come before and who never received such treatment from God?

- Why is it that those that agree with her visions or think she is on the right path are supposedly enlightened by and please God & those who don't simply don't understand her, are vexing her, are with Satan, or haven't been enlightened by God?

- If Jesus supposedly wants sermons on mercy, why did He himself typically speak of judgment rather than mercy? Have not preachers throughout history said that they receive the most conversions when they give sermons on hell? And why

143

would Jesus ask for sermons on mercy precisely when most priests are already silent on hell?

- How are we to accept that there is essentially no corroboration for her alleged experiences? That it's pretty much all based on unproven assertions in her own writings?

- How are we to accept that God picks favorites (e.g. souls that are "particularly dear" and "especially chosen" souls)?

- How are we to believe that Mary & Joseph kept leaving the infant Jesus with Faustina before disappearing?

- Jesus' words and actions in her diary seem out of character based on the biblical portrayal of our Lord - yet Jesus is the same yesterday, today, and forever. So how can we believe Faustina's portrayal of Jesus?

- How is it that Faustina can receive so many extraordinary praises and promises from God and make so few comments in response? Can you imagine the reaction you might have to some of the praise and promises she supposedly received directly from God?

- How is it that Faustina can be so matter-of-fact when Jesus and Mary, etc. talk to her?

- How do we know for sure that her visions are not just delusions / hallucinations / imaginings? Even she herself was not certain of her visions at times.

- In her writings, she mentions her being a 'saint' and not being judged. Wouldn't other saints in their humility have run from such a message, fearing it was a delusion of the devil? Yet, she accepts it all in stride.

- How is it Faustina mentions her suffering so much, but she is yet still able to write so very much?

- By devotees' own admission, in burning her diary, Faustina promptly obeyed the devil - against obedience - who she thought was an angel. Isn't it therefore true that she is not the most trustworthy source concerning her visions? What other saint has a record like this?

- Why does Faustina's version of Mary wear transparent clothing considering that transparent fabric is not modest? Certainly the Mother of God would never dress in an immodest manner!

- Why is it that Faustina says Jesus cannot bear her tears (see Diary, par. 928)? How was he able to bear His Mother's tears during the Passion? Or everyone else's tears throughout history? But not Faustina's?

- Why would Jesus say all that exists is Faustina's?

- Why would Jesus offer to create a new world for Faustina?

- If St. Michael was ordered to take "special care" of Faustina, why was she 'deceived by devil' into burning her diary?

- Why is Faustina's message so often in contrast to what we find in Holy Scripture?

- Why does Faustina make so little mention of people going to Confession for mercy considering that this is precisely the means Jesus established for dispensing mercy to sinners?

- How is it that her version of Jesus impersonates a priest, sits in a chalice, plays on the altar, and rewards Jews who were baptized without their permission? Who can believe this is really Jesus?

- How can we not question the uncharacteristic closeness - even physical closeness - that Faustina claims she has with

Jesus and the Blessed Virgin Mary? Since when are Jesus & Mary huggers?

- When Faustina claims to have seen God the Father, why was there no fear? Compare her reaction with Moses'.

- Why should we not be concerned about a devotion that is almost certain NOT to have received approval if it were not for the direct involvement of (the Koran-kissing, ever-ecumenical) Pope John Paul II? *[Please Note: No disrespect is intended here.]*

- If we just need to trust in and adore God's mercy for salvation, why does Scripture tell us to work out our salvation "with fear and trembling" (see Phil. 2:12)?

- In Scripture, we are told to expect suffering and persecution - yet Faustina's version of Jesus keeps coming to console her when she experiences the slightest suffering. Who ever heard of Jesus being this doting on any other saint - including any of the martyrs who experienced great actual, physical suffering?

How many more issues are needed before YOU see a problem?

+ + +

Note: See Below For Quotations Referenced Above

PART 2

QUOTES REFERENCED ABOVE...

#A1 - CONTRADICTIONS

------- CONTRADICTION -------

She claimed the Blessed Virgin Mary told her those who preserve zealously till death in Her Congregation will be spared purgatory...

> "Towards the end of the ceremony carried out in honor of the Mother of God, I saw the Virgin Mary, and She said to me, Oh, how very pleased I am with the homage of your love! And at that moment She covered all the sisters of our Congregation with Her mantle. With Her right hand, She clasped Mother General Michael to herself, and with Her left hand She did so to me, while all the sisters were at Her feet, covered with Her mantle. Then the Mother of God said, Everyone who perseveres zealously till death in My Congregation will be spared the fire of purgatory, and I desire that each one distinguish herself by the following virtues: humility and meekness; chastity and love of God and neighbor; compassion and mercy." (Diary, par. 1244)

Yet, she reports at least one of the Sisters being in Purgatory...

> "When Sister Dominic died at about one o'clock in the night, she came to me and gave me to know that she was dead. I prayed fervently for her. In the morning, the sisters told me that she was no longer alive, and I replied that I knew, because she had visited me. The sister infirmarian [Sister Chrysostom] asked me to help dress

147

her. And then when I was alone with her, the Lord gave me to know that she was still suffering in purgatory. I redoubled my prayers for her. However, despite the zeal with which I always pray for our deceased sisters, I got mixed up as regards the days, and instead of offering three days of prayer, as the rule directs us to do, by mistake I offered only two days. On the fourth day, she gave me to know that I still owed her prayers, and that she was in need of them. I immediately formed the intention of offering the whole day for her, and not just that day but much more, as love of neighbor dictated to me." (Diary, par. 1382)

------- **CONTRADICTION** -------

She claims "every one of her acts, even the very smallest, will be a delight to God's eyes"...

"And the Lord said to me, You are the delight of My Heart; from today on, every one of your acts, even the very smallest, will be a delight to My eyes, whatever you do. At that moment I felt transconsecrated. My earthly body was the same, but my soul was different; God was now living in it with the totality of His delight. This is not a feeling, but a conscious reality that nothing can obscure." (Diary, par. 137)

But then she also says...

- "Jesus often makes known to me what He does not like in my soul, and He has more than once rebuked me for what seemed to be trifles, but which were, in fact, things of great importance." (Diary, par. 145)

- "I saw that it was not Mother Superior, but the Lord Jesus who looked deeply into me and gave me to understand how painful it was to Him when I did not, even in the smallest things, do my Superior's will, which is My will, [He said]. I

148

asked pardon of the Lord and took the warning very much to heart." (Diary, par. 329)

- "Oh, how much that displeased God! In one moment, the presence of God left me, that great presence of God which is continuously within me in a distinctly felt way. At that moment, however, it completely left me." (Diary, par. 715)

- "At that moment, I heard these words in my soul: This is My faithful servant; he will help you to fulfill My will here on earth. Yet, I did not open myself to him as the Lord wishes. And for some time I struggled against grace. During each confession, God's grace penetrated me in a very special way, yet I did not reveal my soul before him, and I had the intention of not going to confession to that priest. After this decision, a terrible anxiety entered my soul. God reproached me severely." (Diary, par. 263)

- "When Jesus ravished me by His beauty and drew me to Himself, I then saw what in my soul was displeasing to Him and made up my mind to remove it, cost what it may; and aided by the grace of God I did remove it at once." (Diary, par. 293)

- "Know that the faults you commit against him wound My Heart." (Diary, par. 362)

- "Nevertheless, the Lord gave me to know how much this had displeased Him, and I was severely admonished..." (Diary, par. 1383)

------- CONTRADICTION -------

She claims she has no more self concern...

"There is no longer any moment in my life for self concern." (Diary, par. 1662)

Yet she soon after says the following...

"April 19, [1938]. During recreation, one of the sisters [Sister Cajetan] said, 'Sister Faustina is doing so poorly that she can hardly walk, but may she die soon because she is going to be a saint.' Then one of the sister directresses [Sister Casimir] said, 'That she is going to die, we know; but whether she is going to be a saint, that is another question.' There then began some malicious remarks on this subject. I kept silent; then I put in a word, but I saw that the conversation was getting worse, so again I fell silent." (Diary, par. 1672)

"April 20, [1938]. Departure for Pradnik. I was very worried that I would be put in bed in a ward and be exposed to all sorts of things. If it were to be for only a week or two... But it is for such a long time, two months or perhaps more. In the evening, I went in for a long talk with the Lord Jesus. When I saw the Lord Jesus, I poured out my whole heart before Him, all my troubles, fears and apprehensions. Jesus lovingly listened to me and then said, Be at peace, My child, I am with you. Go in great peace. All is ready; I have ordered, in My own special way, a private room to be prepared for you. Reassured and overwhelmed with gratitude, I went to bed." (Diary, par. 1674)

------- **CONTRADICTION** -------

First she says children uphold the world...

"Once, after an adoration for our country, a pain pierced my soul, and I began to pray in this way: 'Most merciful Jesus, I beseech You through the intercession of Your Saints, and especially the intercession of Your dearest Mother who nurtured You from childhood, bless my native land. I beg You, Jesus, look not on our sins, but on the tears of little children, on the hunger and cold

150

they suffer. Jesus, for the sake of these innocent ones, grant me the grace that I am asking of You for my country.' At that moment, I saw the Lord Jesus, His eyes filled with tears, and He said to me, You see, My daughter, what great compassion I have for them. Know that it is they who uphold the world." (Diary, par. 286)

But then says chosen souls "sustain the world in existence"...

"So I turn to you, you – chosen souls... Their number is very small. They are a defense for the world before the justice of the Heavenly Father and a means of obtaining mercy for the world. The love and sacrifice of these souls sustain the world in existence." (Diary, par. 367)

And...

"And the Lord gave me to know who it is that upholds the existence of mankind: it is the chosen souls. When the number of the chosen ones is complete, the world will cease to exist." (Diary, par. 926)

And...

"Today, the Lord gave me knowledge of His anger toward mankind which deserves to have its days shortened because of its sins. But I learned that the world's existence is maintained by chosen souls; that is, the religious orders. Woe to the world when there will be a lack of religious orders!" (Diary, par. 1434)

And also says that Jesus is "gravely" offended by children...

"On one occasion, I saw the convent of the new congregation. As I walked about, inspecting everything, I suddenly saw a crowd of children who seemed to be no older than five to eleven years of age. When they saw me they surrounded me and began to cry out, 'Defend us from evil,' and they led me into the chapel which was in this convent. When I entered the chapel, I saw the distressful Lord Jesus. Jesus looked at me graciously and said that He was gravely offended by children: You are to defend them from evil. From that moment, I have been praying for children, but I feel that prayer alone is not enough." (Diary, par. 765)

------- **CONTRADICTION** -------

She claims she "won't be judged"...

"I heard this voice in my soul: From today on, do not fear God's judgment, for you will not be judged." (Diary, par. 374)

But later she talks about her judgment...

- "Shield me with the omnipotence of Your mercy, and judge me leniently as well." (Diary, par. 1480)

- "O my Jesus, on the day of the last judgment, You will demand from me an account of this work of mercy" (Diary, par. 660)

- "O Jesus, shield me with Your mercy and also judge me leniently, or else Your justice may rightly damn me." (Diary, par. 1093)

------- **CONTRADICTION** -------

She claims Jesus said all creatures always fulfill His will...

"And know this, too, My daughter: all creatures, whether they know it or not, and whether they want to or not, always fulfill My will." (Diary, par. 586)

But then claims action on her part could have thwarted God's plans...

"Action on my part could indeed thwart God's plans"
(Diary, par. 1401)

------- CONTRADICTION -------

She claims that Jesus will not permits souls that are with Him to err...

"I learned that if a soul is with Jesus, He will not permit it to err." (Diary, par. 1503)

But she says that she fell into error...

"It so happened that I fell again into a certain error, in spite of a sincere resolution not to do so" (Diary, par. 1293)

------- CONTRADICTION -------

On November 29th, 1936, she claims the Blessed Virgin Mary was going to obtain for her "the grace of an interior life which will be such that, without ever leaving that interior life" she would be able to carry out all her external duties "with even greater care"...

"The Mother of God has taught me how to prepare for the Feast of Christmas. I saw Her today, without the Infant Jesus. She said to me: My daughter, strive after silence and humility, so that Jesus, who dwells in your heart continuously, may be able to rest. Adore Him in your heart; do not go out from your inmost being. My daughter, I shall obtain for you the grace of an interior life which will be such that, without ever leaving that interior life, you will be able to carry out all your external duties with even greater care[!]. Dwell with

153

Him continuously in your heart. He will be your
strength. Communicate with creatures only in so far as
is necessary and is required by your duties. You are a
dwelling place pleasing to the living God; in you He
dwells continuously with love and delight. And the
living presence of God, which you experience in a more
vivid and distinct way, will confirm you, my daughter,
in the things I have told you. Try to act in this way until
Christmas Day, and then He Himself will make known
to you in what way you will be communing and uniting
yourself with Him." (Diary, par. 785)

**Yet ten days later (December 9th), she leaves to undergo
treatment for three months...**

"Today [December 9, 1936], I am leaving for Pradnik,
just outside Cracow, to undergo treatment. I am to stay
there for three months." (Diary, par. 794)

**Therefore, it is clear that she could not have carried out all her
external duties "with even greater care" - since she wasn't even
there.**

------- CONTRADICTION -------

She says any doubts she has "always" come from outside...

"Something was pervading my whole being, and yet I
feared being deluded. However, these doubts always
came from outside, because in the depths of my soul I
felt it was the Lord who was penetrating my being ...
But these doubts always come from without, a fact
which inclined me to close myself up more and more
within myself. When, during confession, I sense
uncertainty on the part of the priest, I do not open my
soul to its depths, but only accuse myself of my sins."
(Diary, par. 74-75)

154

Yet she also says things like...

- "Once again, a terrible darkness envelops my soul. It seems to me that I am falling prey to illusions." (Diary, par. 211)

- "On the fourth day, doubts began to trouble me; Is not this tranquility of mine false?" (Diary, par. 229)

- "In the evening during benediction, such thoughts as these began to distress me: Is not perhaps all this that I am saying about God's great mercy just a lie or an illusion...?" (Diary, par. 359)

- "I myself began to waver" (Diary, par. 112)

- "Although the temptations are strong, a whole wave of doubts beats against my soul, and discouragement stands by, ready to enter into the act." (Diary, par. 1086)

- Etc.

------- **CONTRADICTION** -------

She claims that Jesus said it would cause Him pain if she left her convent and that it was to that place God called her and "nowhere else"...

"After a while a brightness filled my cell, and on the curtain I saw the very sorrowful Face of Jesus. There were open wounds on His Face, and large tears were falling on my bedspread. Not knowing what all this meant, I asked Jesus, 'Jesus, who has hurt You so?' And Jesus said to me, It is you who will cause Me this pain if you leave this convent. It is to this place that I called you and nowhere else; and I have prepared many graces for you. I begged pardon of Jesus and immediately changed my decision." (Diary, par. 19)

But later she says...

- "The Lord visited my cell today and said to me, My daughter, I will not leave you in this community for much longer. I am telling you this so that you will be more diligent in taking advantage of the graces which I grant you." (Diary, par. 776)

- "As I was walking in the garden in the evening, I heard these words: By your entreaties, you and your companions shall obtain mercy for yourselves and for the world. I understood that I would not remain in the Congregation in which I am at the present time." (Diary, par. 435)

- "Up to now, I have been wondering, with some fear, where these inspirations would lead me. My fear increased when the Lord made known to me that I was to leave this Congregation." (Diary, par. 1263)

- "At the very beginning of Holy Mass on the following day, I saw Jesus in all His unspeakable beauty. He said to me that he desired that such a Congregation be founded as soon as possible, and you shall live in it together with your companions. My Spirit shall be the rule of your life. Your life is to be modeled on Mine, from the crib to My death on the Cross. Penetrate My mysteries, and you will know the abyss of My mercy towards creatures and My unfathomable goodness – and this you shall make known to the world. Through your prayers, you shall mediate between heaven and earth." (Diary, par. 438)

#A2 - FACTUAL ERRORS / INACCURACIES

Examples...

- She gets her vision of the Ascension wrong (see above)

156

- She writes, "I learned that if a soul is with Jesus, He will not permit it to err." (Diary, par. 1503) - Yet, souls that are with Jesus err all the time (even the Pope can err when not speaking infallibly)

- She says "My fear increased when the Lord made known to me that I was to leave this Congregation" (Diary, par. 1263) - Yet she was never to leave the Congregation

- She claims "These difficulties prove that this work is [God's]" (Diary, par. 1295) - Yet, difficulties do not necessarily prove that a work is God's. Rather, the Holy Spirit removing difficulties may actually be proof that a work is God's

- She speaks of angels and "their time of mercy" (Diary, par. 1489) - Yet, angels didn't have a 'time of mercy'

- She asks, "Jesus Crucified, transform my weakness into omnipotence." (Diary, par. 1151) - Yet a mere human cannot have omnipotence

- She writes, "At that moment, such profound gratitude to God was awakened in my soul that I burst into tears of joy like a little child. I prepared to receive Holy Communion next morning as 'viaticum,' and I said the prayers of the dying for my own intention." (Diary, par. 1551) - Yet, she didn't die for many months after this

- She says she was told not to rely on creatures "even in the smallest things, because this displeases [God]" (Diary, par. 295) - Yet, how can humans not rely on creatures even in the smallest things? We have to - God set things up this way!

- She claims that in Christ's atoning sacrifice "mercy triumphed over justice" (Diary, par. 1572) - Yet in reality, both were satisfied

- She says that the Holy Trinity "cannot love a soul which is stained with sin" (Diary, par. 1728) - Yet scripture says "But God proves his love for us in that while we were still sinners Christ died for us." (Rom. 5:8)

- She claims she was taught a chaplet in which one is to say "one OUR FATHER and HAIL MARY and the I BELIEVE IN GOD" (Diary, par. 476) - Yet the "I believe in God" prayer is actually called the Creed (why would God fail to use the correct term for the prayer?)

- She has a mistaken view of the battle in heaven that occurred before human beings were created (and therefore before God's mercy was ever dispensed). She claims the battle in heaven was over an angel not recognizing God's (not yet exercised!) mercy, rather than the well-known battle cry of Lucifer: "I will not serve". She writes: "One of the most beautiful spirits would not recognize Your [not yet exercised!] mercy, And, blinded by his pride, he drew others after him. Angel of great beauty, he became Satan And was cast down in one moment from heaven's heights into hell. Then the faithful spirits cried, 'Glory to God's mercy!'[!] And they stood firm in spite of the fiery test. Glory to Jesus, the Christ abased [abased before He ever became Incarnate?], Glory to His Mother, the humble and pure Virgin [although the Blessed Virgin Mary was not yet Christ's mother - she was not even born yet (in fact, no human beings existed at this point)]. After this battle, the pure spirits plunged into the ocean of Divinity; Contemplating and praising the depths of His mercy [contemplating His mercy which hadn't yet been exercised?], They drown in His mercy and manifold light, Possessing in knowledge the Trinity of persons, the Oneness of Godhead." (Diary, par. 1742)

- She seems to confuse love and mercy: "O God, who are happiness in Your very self and have no need of creatures to make You happy, because of Yourself You are the fullness of love; yet, out of Your fathomless mercy [love!] You call creatures into being and grant them a share in Your eternal happiness and in Your life, that divine indwelling life which You live, One God in Three Persons. In Your unfathomable mercy [love!], You have created angelic spirits and admitted them to Your love and to Your divine intimacy. You have made them capable of eternal love. Although You bestowed on them so generously, O Lord, the splendor of love and beauty, Your fullness was not diminished in the least, O God, nor have their love and beauty completed You, because You are everything in Yourself. And if You have allowed them to participate in Your happiness and to exist and to love You, that is only due to the abyss of Your mercy [love!]. This is Your unfathomable goodness, for which they glorify You without end, humbling themselves at the feet of Your majesty as they chant their eternal hymn: Holy, Holy, Holy..." (Diary, par. 1741)

#A3 - EXAGGERATIONS

Examples...

- "I cannot keep this happiness locked in my own heart alone, for His flames burn Me and cause my bosom and my entrails to burst asunder." (Diary, par. 491)

- "I see your love so pure, purer than that of the angels" (Diary, par. 1061)

- "This is a martyrdom beyond description" (Diary, par. 856) *[A martyrdom, yet she is able to write? And there is no blood?]*

- "Nevertheless, such an extraordinary disgust with life came over me that I had to make a great act of the will to consent to go on living" (Diary, par. 1497)

159

- "I felt the separation of my spirit from my body." (Diary, par. 439) *[This would be DEATH]*

- "O Lord, deify my actions so that they will merit eternity" (Diary, par. 1371)

- "Divinize me so that my deeds may have supernatural value." (Diary, par. 1242)

- "I am a white host before you, O Divine priest. Consecrate me Yourself, and may my transubstantiation [!] be known only to You" (Diary, par. 1564)

- "You are a fount which makes all creatures [animals, insects, trees?] happy by Your infinite mercy." (Diary, par. 793)

- "In spite of Satan's anger, The Divine Mercy will triumph over the whole world and will be worshipped by all [!] souls." (Diary, par. 1789)

Note: Also see Faustina/Dramatic below

#A4 - PROPHECIES THAT DO NOT MATERIALIZE

According to Holy Scripture, prophecies that do not materialize did NOT come from God...

> **Deut. 18:21-22: "If you say to yourselves, 'How can we recognize an oracle which the Lord has spoken?', know that, even though a prophet speaks in the name of the Lord, if his oracle is not fulfilled or verified, it is an oracle which the Lord did not speak."**

------- **FALSE PROPHECY #1** -------

Her diary states...

"At the very beginning of Holy Mass on the following day, I saw Jesus in all His unspeakable beauty. He said to me that he desired that such a Congregation be founded as soon as possible, and you shall live in it together with your companions. My Spirit shall be the rule of your life. Your life is to be modeled on Mine, from the crib to My death on the Cross. Penetrate My mysteries, and you will know the abyss of My mercy towards creatures and My unfathomable goodness – and this you shall make known to the world. Through your prayers, you shall mediate between heaven and earth." (Diary, par. 438)

And...

"The Lord visited my cell today and said to me, My daughter, I will not leave you in this community for much longer. I am telling you this so that you will be more diligent in taking advantage of the graces which I grant you." (Diary, par. 776)

And...

"As I was walking in the garden in the evening, I heard these words: By your entreaties, you and your companions shall obtain mercy for yourselves and for the world. I understood that I would not remain in the Congregation in which I am at the present time." (Diary, par. 435)

And...

"Up to now, I have been wondering, with some fear, where these inspirations would lead me. My fear increased when the Lord made known to me that I was to leave this Congregation." (Diary, par. 1263)

Yet, she did NOT live to see the congregation founded, nor did she ever live in it.

------- **FALSE PROPHECY #2** -------

Her diary states...

> "The Lord Jesus appeared as He was during the scourging. In His hands He was holding a white garment with which He clothed me and a cord with which He girded me, and He covered me with a red cloak like the one He was clothed with during His Passion and a veil of the same color, and He said to me, This is how you and your companions are going to be clothed." (Diary, par. 526)

Yet, she did NOT live to see the congregation founded, nor wear its garb.

------- **FALSE PROPHECY #3** -------

Her diary states...

> "March 23, 1937. Today is the seventh day of the novena. I have received a great and inconceivable grace: the Most Merciful Jesus has promised that I will be present at the celebration of this solemn Feast." (Diary, par. 1042)

Yet, she died the following year, before the feast was approved. [Note: In her diary, we know on 1/6/38 or later it was being considered, but was not yet in place and would not be in place until after her death (see par. 1463, 1530, 1680)]

#A5 - SCANDALOUS ACTIONS

Forced baptism of adult Jewish woman: (also see above)

"This day is so special for me; even though I
encountered so many sufferings, my soul is overflowing
with great joy. In a private room next to mine, there was
a Jewish woman who was seriously ill. I went to see her
three days ago and was deeply pained at the thought that
she would soon die without having her soul cleansed by
the grace of Baptism. I had an understanding with her
nurse, a [religious] Sister, that when her last moment
would be approaching, she would baptize her. There
was this difficulty however, that there were always
some Jewish people with her. However, I felt inspired to
pray before the image which Jesus had instructed me to
have painted. I have a leaflet with the Image of the
divine Mercy on the cover. And I said to the Lord,
'Jesus, You Yourself told me that You would grant
many graces through this image. I ask You, then, for the
grace of Holy Baptism for this Jewish lady. It makes no
difference who will baptize her, as long as she is
baptized.'

After these words, I felt strangely at peace, and I was
quite sure that, despite the difficulties, the waters of
Holy Baptism would be poured upon her soul. That
night, when she was very low, I got out of bed three
times to see her, watching for the right moment to give
her this grace. The next morning, she seemed to feel a
little better. In the afternoon her last moment began to
approach. The Sister who was her nurse said that
Baptism would be difficult because they were with her.
The moment came when the sick woman began to lose
consciousness, and as a result, in order to save her, they
began to run about; some [went] to fetch the doctor,
while others went off in other directions to find help.

And so the patient was left alone, and Sister baptized her, and before they had all rushed back, her soul was beautiful, adorned with God's grace. Her final agony began immediately, but it did not last long. It was as if she fell asleep. All of a sudden, I saw her soul ascending to heaven in wondrous beauty. Oh, how beautiful is a soul with sanctifying grace! Joy flooded my heart that before this image I had received so great a grace for this soul.

Oh, how great is God's mercy; let every soul praise it. O my Jesus, that soul for all eternity will be singing You a hymn of mercy. I shall not forget the impression this day has made on my soul. This is the second great grace which I have received here for souls before this image.

Oh, how good the Lord is, and how full of compassion; Jesus, how heartily I thank You for these graces."
(Diary, par. 916-917)

[Note: See above for notes]

Seemingly sacrilegious confession: (also see above)

"A certain person seems to have made it her task to try out my virtue in all sorts of ways. One day, she stopped me in the corridor and began by saying that she had no grounds for rebuking me, but she ordered me to stand there opposite the small chapel for half an hour and to wait for Mother Superior, who was to pass by there after recreation, and I was to accuse myself of various things which she had told me to say. Although I had no idea of these things being on my soul, I was obedient and waited for Mother Superior for a full half hour. Each sister who passed by looked at me with a smile. When I accused myself before Mother Superior [Raphael], she sent me to my confessor. When I made my confession, the priest saw immediately that this was something that

164

did not come from my own soul and that I had not the faintest idea of such things. He was very surprised that this person had dared to take upon herself to give such orders." (Diary, par. 196)

[Note: See above for notes]

Faustina's self-admitted lying/misrepresenting herself:

"I often [!] represented myself to my superiors other than I was in reality and spoke of miseries of which I had no notion." (Diary, par. 1503)

#A6 - THEOLOGICAL PROBLEMS / FAULTY THEOLOGY

Examples...

- Mercy depending on trust rather than sorrow for sins (see above)

- God's 'greatest attribute' (see above)

- Sinners' supposed 'right to mercy' (see above)

- Everyone fulfills His will (see above)

- Various other items (see above)

Also...

- The idea that Faustina has "first place among the virgins" (Diary, par. 282) with no mention of the Blessed Virgin Mary

- The idea that God united himself more closely with Faustina "than with any other creature" (Diary, par. 1546) - again with no mention of the Blessed Virgin Mary

- The idea that God is wounded more by things that aren't sins than by sins (e.g. "My daughter, that once glance of yours directed at someone else would wound Me more than many sins committed by another person", Diary, par. 588)

- The idea that Faustina's chastity could be "greater than that of the angels" (Diary, par. 534)

- The impression that God may impede our free will [e.g. "But when the day for confession came, I prepared a whole mass of those sins of which I was to accuse myself. However, in the confessional, God allowed me to accuse myself of only two imperfections, despite my efforts to make a confession according to what I had prepared." (Diary, par. 1802) And "Human plans will be thwarted, since they must conform to My will." (Diary, par. 1180)]

- The false & dangerous idea that bad actions are not bad based on intentions: "A moral principle. If one does not know what is better, one must reflect, consider and seek advice, because one must not act with an uncertain conscience. When uncertain, say to yourself: 'Whatever I do will be good. I have the intention of doing good.' The Lord God accepts what we consider good, and the Lord God also accepts and considers it as good. *[WRONG!]* One should not worry if, after some time, one sees that these things are not good. *[WRONG!]* God looks at the intention with which we begin, and will reward us accordingly. This is a principle which we ought to follow." (Diary, par. 800) *[Note: This is obviously not true. Jesus tells us that if the bind lead the blind, both will fall into the pit (Mt. 15:14). There is no mention here of their good intentions. He also tells us that one ignorant of his master's will may be still beaten (Lk. 12:48). God isn't relativistic and something that is inherently bad cannot be*

166

made good by a good intention. If anything, one may perhaps be spared punishment for something bad if the intention was truly good/innocent, but this is far from God regarding a bad action as a good one!]

#A7 - BAD / DANGEROUS ADVICE

Examples...

- **Not calling priests for the dying as we are instructed in Holy Scripture (rather than mentioning getting a priest to dispense extreme unction, her diary recommends praying a chaplet)...**

"When I entered my solitude, I heard these words: At the hour of their death, I defend as My own glory every soul that will say this chaplet; or when others say it for a dying person, the indulgence is the same. When this chaplet is said by the bedside of a dying person, God's anger is placated, unfathomable mercy envelops the soul, and the very depths of My tender mercy are moved for the sake of the sorrowful Passion of My Son." (Diary, par. 811)

"When I entered the chapel for a moment, the Lord said to me, My daughter, help Me to save a certain dying sinner. Say the chaplet that I have taught you for him. When I began to say the chaplet, I saw the man dying in the midst of terrible torment and struggle. His Guardian Angel was defending him, but he was, as it were, powerless against the enormity of the soul's misery. A multitude of devils was waiting for the soul. But while I was saying the chaplet, I saw Jesus just as He is depicted in the image. The rays which issued from Jesus' Heart enveloped the sick man, and the powers of darkness fled in panic. The sick man peacefully breathed his last. When I came to myself, I understood how very important the chaplet was for the dying. It appeases the anger of God." (Diary, par. 1565)

- **About presumption (see above)**

- **About following interior inspirations...**

"When I entered my own cell, my soul was engulfed by the great love of God, and I understood that we should take great heed of our interior inspirations and follow them faithfully, and that faithfulness to one grace draws down others." (Diary, par. 756)

[Note that we can easily be lead astray by 'interior inspirations' (as Faustina herself admits), especially if one does not have a well-formed conscience.]

#A8 - DISTURBING IMAGES

Examples...

- "After a while, I saw the Child Jesus on the altar, joyfully and playfully holding out His hands to him. But a moment later the priest took the beautiful Child into his hands, broke Him up and ate Him alive." (Diary, par. 312)

- "Once I saw a big crowd of people in our chapel, in front of the chapel and in the street, because there was no room for them inside. The chapel was decorated for a feast. There were a lot of clergy near the altar, and then our sisters and those of many other congregations. They were all waiting for the person who was to take a place on the altar. Suddenly I heard a voice saying that I was to take the place on the altar. But as soon as I left the corridor to go across the yard and enter the chapel, following the voice that was calling me, all the people began to throw at me whatever they had to hand: mud, stones, sand, brooms, to such an extent that I at first hesitated to go forward. But the voice kept on calling me even more earnestly, so I walked on bravely. When I entered the chapel, the superiors, the sisters, the students, and even my parents started to hit me with whatever they could, and so whether I wanted to or not, I quickly took my place [!] on the altar. As soon as I was there, the very same people, the students, the sisters, the superiors and my parents all began to hold their arms out to me asking for graces" (Diary, par. 31)

- "December 25, [1936]. Midnight Mass. During Mass, God's presence pierced me through and through. A moment before the Elevation I saw the Mother of God and the Infant Jesus and the good Old Man [St. Joseph]. The Most Holy Mother spoke these words to me: My daughter, Faustina, take this most precious Treasure, and she gave me the Infant Jesus. When I took Jesus in my arms, my soul felt such unspeakable joy that I am unable to describe it. But, strange thing, after a short while Jesus became awful, horrible-looking, grown up and suffering; and then the vision vanished, and soon it was time to go to Holy Communion." (Diary, par. 846)

- "Midnight Mass. As Holy Mass began, I immediately felt a great interior recollection; joy filled my soul. During the offertory, I saw Jesus on the altar, incomparably beautiful. The whole time the Infant kept looking at everyone, stretching out his little hands. During the elevation, the Child was not looking towards the chapel but up to heaven. After the elevation, He looked at us again, but just for a short while, because He was broken up and eaten by the priest in the usual manner." (Diary, par. 347)

- "One day, after our Mass, I suddenly saw my confessor [Father Sopocko] saying Mass in Saint Michael's Church, in front of the picture of the Mother of God. It was at the time of the Offertory, and I saw the Infant Jesus clinging to him as if fleeing from something and seeking refuge [!] in him. But when the time came for Holy Communion, He disappeared as usual. Suddenly, I saw the Blessed Mother, who shielded him with her cloak and said, Courage, My son, courage. She said something else which I could not hear." (Diary, par. 597)

- Etc.

#A9 - AN INCONCEIVABLE ATTEMPT TO IMPOSE NEW DOCTRINE / PROMOTE DANGEROUS PRACTICES

For example...

- Threatens hell for those who do not adore God's in mercy (see above)

- Call to trust in mercy as an apparent substitute for repentance (see above)

- Claim that mercy is God's "greatest attribute" (see above)

- Claims that the greater the sinner, the greater 'right' he has to mercy (instead of having a greater right to punishment) (see above)

- Discouraging fear of the Lord (see above)

- Gives false hope that there are shortcuts which will allow some persons to avoid judgment - e.g. those persons who glorify God's mercy and spread its worship or who venerate an image (see above)

- Various others (see above)

#A10 - UNCHARACTERISTIC BEHAVIOR & SPEECH ATTRIBUTED TO GOD, THE BLESSED VIRGIN MARY, ETC.

Examples...

Uncharacteristic way they supposedly talk...

- "During one conference, Jesus said to me, You are a sweet grape in a chosen cluster; I want others to have a share in the juice that is flowing within you." (Diary, par. 393)

- "Your sincere love is as pleasing to My Heart as the fragrance of a rosebud at morningtide, before the sun has taken the dew from it. The freshness of your heart captivates Me; that is why I united Myself with you more closely than with any other creature" (Diary, par. 1546)

- "Tell aching mankind to snuggle close to My merciful Heart" (Diary, par. 1074) *[Jesus really says "snuggle close"? Can you picture the Jesus in scripture saying this? Or any man outside of an intimate relationship?]*

- "Do you think that I will not have enough omnipotence to support you?" (Diary, par. 527)

- "When Jesus entered this light, I heard these words, Write down at once what you hear: I am the Lord in My essence and am immune to orders or needs." (Diary, par. 85)

- "I understand you because I am God-Man." (Diary, par. 797)

- "I am concerned about every beat of your heart. Every stirring of your love is reflected in My Heart. I thirst for your love." (Diary, par. 1542)

- "When I received Holy Communion, I said to Him, 'Jesus, I thought about You so many times last night,' and Jesus answered me, And I thought of you before I called you into being. 'Jesus, in what way were You thinking about me?' In terms of admitting you to My eternal happiness." (Diary, par. 1292)

- "Know that you are now on a great stage where all heaven and earth are watching you." (Diary, par. 1760)

- "Today, I heard these words: Know, my child, that for your sake I grant blessings to this whole vicinity. But you ought to thank Me on their behalf, as they do not thank Me for the kindnesses I extend to them. For the sake of your gratitude, I will continue to bless them." (Diary, par. 719) *[Thank on someone else's behalf? In Scripture, Jesus didn't tell the man who returned to offer his appreciation to also thank Him on behalf of the others who didn't return to think Him!]*

- "That evening Jesus said to me, I want you to stay home." (Diary, par. 64)

- "All is ready; I have ordered, in My own special way, a private room to be prepared for you." (Diary, par. 1674)

- "And your compassion, within the bounds of obedience, has pleased Me, and this is why I came down from My throne – to taste the fruits of your mercy." (Diary, par. 1312)

- "I saw the Lord Jesus leaning over me, and He asked, My daughter, what are you writing?" (Diary, par. 1693)

- "Jesus stood by my side and said. My daughter, what are you thinking about right now?" (Diary, par. 960)

- "Today, the Lord said to me, My daughter, I am told that there is much simplicity in you, so why do you not tell Me about everything that concerns you, even the smallest details?" (Diary, par. 921)

- "This evening, Jesus said to me, My daughter, do you need anything?" (Diary, par. 1682)

- "Suddenly Jesus stood before me and said, What are you doing here so early?" (Diary, par. 1705)

- "This evening, the Lord asked me, Do you not have any desires in your heart?" (Diary, par. 1700)

- "And the Lord looked at me with love and said, And what is it that you desire to tell Me?" (Diary, par. 873)

Uncharacteristic physical closeness...

- "She [the Blessed Virgin Mary] pressed me to Her Heart" (Diary, par. 1415)

- "I saw the Lord, who clasped to me to His Heart" (Diary, par. 928)

- "Now, rest your head on My bosom, on My heart" (Diary, par. 36)

- "Jesus pressed me to His Heart" (Diary, par. 853)

- "I saw Jesus in the usual way, and He spoke these words to me: Lay your head on My shoulder, rest and regain your strength. I am always with you." (Diary, par. 498)

- "At that moment, the Child Jesus was standing by me on the side of my kneeler, and He leaned with His two little hands against my shoulder, gracious and joyful, His look deep and penetrating." (Diary, par. 434)

- "I nestled close to the Most Sacred Heart of Jesus" (Diary, par. 1318)

- "Jesus gave me His hand, sat me at His side, and said with kindness, My bride, you always please Me by your humility." (Diary, par. 1563)

- "During Holy Mass, I saw the Lord, who said to me, Lean your head on My breast and rest. The Lord pressed me to His Heart..." (Diary, par. 1053)

- "Today, the Lord visited me, pressed me to His Heart and said, Rest, My little child, I am always with you." (Diary, par. 1011)

- "Then I saw the Blessed Virgin, unspeakably beautiful. She came down from the altar [!] to my kneeler, held me close to herself and said to me..." (Diary, par. 449)

- "I followed my confessor's advice, and at the first meeting with the Lord, I fell at Jesus' feet and, with a grief-stricken heart, apologized for everything. Then Jesus lifted me up from the ground and sat me beside Him and let me put my head on His breast, so that I could better understand and feel the desires of His most sweet Heart." (Diary, par. 431)

- "Suddenly, I saw the Lord in His inexpressible beauty. He looked at me graciously and said, My daughter, I too came down from heaven out of love for you; I lived for you, I died for you, and I created the heavens for you. And Jesus pressed me to His Heart and said to me, Very soon now; be at peace, My daughter." (Diary, par. 853)

- "Today during Holy Mass, I saw the Infant Jesus near my kneeler. He appeared to be about one year old, and He asked me to take Him in my arms. When I did take Him in my arms, He cuddled up close to my bosom and said, It is good for Me to be close to your heart." (Diary, par. 1481)

Transparent clothing / uncovered head...

- "In the midst of a great brilliance, I saw the Mother of God clothed in a white gown, girt about with a golden cincture; and there were tiny stars, also of gold, over the whole garment, and chevron-shaped sleeves lined with gold. Her cloak was sky-blue, lightly thrown over the shoulders. A transparent veil was delicately drawn over her head, while her flowing hair was set off beautifully by a golden crown which terminated in little crosses. On Her left arm She held the Child Jesus. A Blessed Mother of this type I had not yet seen. Then She looked at me kindly and said: I am the Mother of God of Priests. At that, She lowered Jesus from her arm to the ground, raised Her right hand heavenward and said: O God, bless Poland, bless priests. Then She addressed me once again: Tell the priests what you have seen. I resolved that at the first opportunity [I would have] of seeing Father [Andrasz] I would tell" (Diary, par. 1585)

- "After these words, my soul was filled with unusual trust. The Mother of God was clothed in a white dress, strangely white, transparent; on Her shoulders She had a transparent blue; that is, a blue-like mantle; with uncovered head [and] flowing hair, She was exquisite, and inconceivably beautiful. She was looking at Father with great tenderness, but after a moment, He broke up this beautiful Child, and living blood flowed forth. Father bent forward and received the true and living Jesus into himself. Had he eaten Him? I do not know how this took place. Jesus, Jesus, I cannot keep up with You, for in an instant, You become incomprehensible to me." (Diary, par. 677)

- "At the beginning of Holy Mass, I saw Jesus in the usual way. He blessed us and then entered the tabernacle. Then I saw the Mother of God in a white garment and blue mantle, with Her head uncovered [! - Uncovered head at Mass!]. She approached me from the altar [!], touched me with Her hands and covered me with Her mantle, saying, Offer these vows

175

for Poland. Pray for her. This was on August fifteen." (Diary, par. 468)

Calling a female 'Apostle' (see above)

Strange requests...

- "Jesus listened to my words with gravity and kindness and spoke these words to me: Tell your confessor that I commune with your soul in such an intimate manner because you do not steal My gifts, and this is why I pour all these graces upon your soul, because I know that you will not hoard them for yourself." (Diary, par. 1069)

- "I heard these words: Tell the Superior General to count on you as the most faithful daughter in the Order." (Diary, par. 1130) *[She is really supposed to say this to her superior? And this as she is preparing to leave the order!]*

- "At that moment, Jesus suddenly stood before me, coming I know not from where, radiant with unbelievable beauty, clothed in a white garment, with uplifted arms, and He spoke these words to me, My daughter, your heart is My repose; it is My delight. I find in it everything that is refused Me by so many souls. Tell this to My representative." (Diary, par. 339) *[She is seriously supposed to tell this to God's representative?]*

- "On one occasion I saw two sisters who were about to enter hell. A terrible agony tore my soul; I prayed to God for them, and Jesus said to me, Go to Mother Superior and tell her that those two sisters are in danger of committing a mortal sin. The next day I told this to the Superior." (Diary, par. 43) *[She was supposed to be a 'tattle tale' even in advance of the sin being committed? What about protecting their good names?]*

'Taking her heart'

"Once, on Christmas Day [1928], I felt the omnipotence and the presence of God surrounding me. And once more I fled from this interior meeting with the Lord. I asked Mother Superior for permission to go to Jozefinek to visit the sisters there. The Superior gave us permission, and we started to get ready right after lunch. The other sisters were already waiting for me at the door of the convent while I ran to my cell to get my cloak. On my way back, as I was passing close to the little chapel, I saw Jesus standing in the doorway. He said to me, Go ahead, but I am taking your heart. Suddenly I felt that I had no heart in my chest. But the sisters were scolding me for lingering behind, saying that it was already getting late, so I quickly went along with them. But a sense of uneasiness troubled me, and a strange longing invaded my soul, through no one knew what was happening except God. After we had been at Jozefinek for only a few minutes, I said to the sisters, 'Let's go back home.' The sisters asked for at least a moment's rest, but my spirit could find no peace. I explained that we must return before dark; and in as much as we had quite a distance to go, we immediately returned home. When Mother Superior met us in the hallway she asked me, 'Haven't the sisters gone yet, or have they already returned?' I said that we had already returned because I did not want to be returning in the evening. I took off my cloak and immediately went to the little chapel. As soon as I entered Jesus said to me, Go to Mother Superior and tell her that you came back, not in order to reach home before dark, but because I had taken your heart[!]. Even though this was very difficult for me, I went to the Superior, and I told her frankly the real reason why I had come back so soon, and I asked pardon of the Lord for everything that had displeased Him. And then Jesus filled me with great joy. I understood that apart from God there is no contentment anywhere" (Diary, par. 42)

Are we really supposed to believe Jesus talks & acts like this? Seriously, taking a heart? - Are we really supposed to believe Jesus would want her to look like a fool? Furthermore, was she not honest about the reason she first gave?

Tasking her with instructing superiors and priests (see above)

Mary supposedly having to be coerced into telling Faustina what she already wanted to tell her...

> "Once, the Mother of God came to visit me. She was sad. Her eyes were cast down. She made it clear that She wanted to say something, and yet, on the other hand, it was as if She did not want to speak to me about it. When I understood this, I began to beg the Mother of God to tell me and to look at me. Just then Mary looked at me with a warm smile and said, You are going to experience certain sufferings because of an illness and the doctors; you will also suffer much because of the image, but do not be afraid of anything. The next day I fell ill and suffered a great deal, just as the Mother of God had told me. But my soul was ready for the sufferings. Suffering is a constant companion of my life." (Diary, par. 316) *[Seriously, she had to 'beg' Mary to tell her? Mary didn't have any problem telling the little children at Fatima that they would suffer!]*

Also...

- Jesus supposedly running and playing on the altar (see above)

- God supposedly being reluctant to exercise justice (see above)

- The Virgin Mary & St. Joseph supposedly leaving the infant Jesus with Faustina and then disappearing (see above)

178

- Etc.

#A11 - FANCIFUL DESCRIPTIONS THAT DO NOT SEEM POSSIBLE IN THE LITERAL SENSE

Examples...

- "I cannot keep this happiness locked in my own heart alone, for His flames burn Me and cause my bosom and my entrails to burst asunder." (Diary, par. 491)

- "The flames of mercy are burning Me" (Diary, par. 1074) *[Really, burning?]*

- "You know very well, O Jesus, that I am constantly swooning because of my longing for You." (Diary, par. 969) *[Constantly swooning?]*

- "My spirit was flooded with light, and my body participated in this as well." (Diary, par. 627) *[How could her body be participating? Was she glowing?]*

- "Then I heard an angel who sang out my whole life history and everything it comprised. I was surprised, but also strengthened." (Diary, par. 1202) *[Wouldn't that take a long time to sing out her whole life history and "everything it comprised"?]*

- "After Holy Communion, I saw Jesus in the same way in my heart and felt Him physically in my heart throughout the day." (Diary, par. 434)

- "I suddenly saw a ciborium with the Blessed Sacrament. The ciborium was uncovered and quite filled with hosts. From the ciborium came a voice: These hosts have been received by souls converted through your prayer and suffering." (Diary, par. 709) *[If they had been received, how could she see still them? Also, how could a voice come from the ciborium?]*

- "most sweet Jesus, who have graciously demanded that I tell the whole world of Your incomprehensible mercy, this day I take into my hands the two rays that spring from Your merciful Heart; that is, the Blood and the Water; and I scatter them all over the globe..." (Diary, par. 836) *[She can scatter them all over the globe from one location?]*

- "At four o'clock when I came for adoration, I saw one of our wards offending God greatly by sins of impure thoughts." (Diary, par. 349) *[How can she see impure thoughts?]*

- "Adore Him in your heart; do not go out from your inmost being." (Diary, par. 785) *[Do not go out from your inmost being? How to do this?]*

- "In one instant the Lord gave me a knowledge of the sins committed throughout the whole world during these days." (Diary, par. 926) *[How would it be possible for the human mind to process such vast knowledge? And why would God give her such knowledge?]*

- "Unceasingly greeting the Mother of God and entering into Her spirit, I begged Her to teach me true love of God. And then I heard these words: I will share with you the secret of My happiness this night during Holy Mass." (Diary, par. 346) *[How did Faustina greet Mary unceasingly and how did Faustina enter into Mary's spirit?]*

- "Though I was hardly aware of it [!], my spirit was drowned in God." (Diary, par. 346) *[How can one's spirit be 'drowned in God' & how could such a one be "hardly aware of it"?]*

- "One day, after Holy Communion, I suddenly saw the Infant Jesus standing by my kneeler and holding on to it with His two little hands." (Diary, par. 566) *[How is the infant standing? Definition of infant: "A very young child (birth to 1 year) who has not yet begun to walk or talk"]*

- "It was such a great suffering that it prevented me from making even the slightest movement; I could not even swallow my saliva. This lasted for about three hours." (Diary, par. 696) *[Is it possible to last like this for 3 hours? Try lasting for 30 minutes!]*

- "One evening, one of the deceased sisters, who had already visited me a few times, appeared to me. The first time I had seen her, she had been in great suffering, and then gradually these sufferings had diminished; this time she was radiant with happiness, and she told me she was already in heaven. She told me that God had tried our house with tribulation because Mother General [Michael] had given in to doubts, not believing what I had said about this soul. And further, as a sign that she only now was in heaven, God would bless our house. Then she came closer to me, embraced me sincerely and said, 'I must go now.' I understood how closely the three stages of a soul's life are bound together; that is to say, life on earth, in purgatory and in heaven [the Communion of Saints]." (Diary, par. 594) *[How is it that Faustina could embrace a dead person when dead people no longer have bodies?]*

- Etc.

#B - FAUSTINA'S VERSION OF JESUS

In contrast to the known Jesus (who is the same "yesterday, today, and forever"- Heb. 13:8), her version of Jesus is...

» doting / attentive / "captivated" - for example, consider these passages...

- "Jesus said to me, You will not be alone, because I am with you always and everywhere. Near to My Heart, fear nothing. I Myself am the cause of your departure. Know that My eyes follow every move of your heart with great attention." (Diary, par. 797)

- "At that moment Jesus asked me, My child, how is your retreat going? I answered, 'But Jesus, You know how it is going.' Yes, I know, but I want to hear it from your own lips and from your heart." (Diary, par. 295)

- "Today, the Lord said to me, My daughter, I am told that there is much simplicity in you, so why do you not tell Me about everything that concerns you, even the smallest details? Tell Me about everything, and know that this will give Me great joy. I answered, 'But You know about everything, Lord.' And Jesus replied to me, Yes, I do know; but you should not excuse yourself with the fact that I know, but with childlike simplicity talk to Me about everything, for My ears and heart are inclined towards you, and your words are dear to Me." (Diary, par. 921)

- "I was very worried that I would be put in bed in a ward and be exposed to all sorts of things. If it were to be for only a week or two... But it is for such a long time, two months or perhaps more. In the evening, I went in for a long talk with the Lord Jesus. When I saw the Lord Jesus, I poured out my whole heart before Him, all my troubles, fears and apprehensions. Jesus lovingly listened to me and then said, Be at peace, My child, I am with you. Go in great peace. All is ready; I have ordered, in My own special way, a private room to be prepared for you. Reassured and overwhelmed with gratitude, I went to bed." (Diary, par. 1674)

- "Tell me all, My child, hide nothing from Me, because My loving Heart, the Heart of your Best Friend, is listening to you." (Diary, par. 1486)

- "I heard these words: My daughter, I am always with you. I have given you the opportunity to practice deeds of mercy which you will perform according to obedience. You will give Me much pleasure if, each evening, you will speak to Me especially about this task." (Diary, par. 1267)

- "I am delighted with your love. Your sincere love is as pleasing to My Heart as the fragrance of a rosebud at morningtide, before the sun has taken the dew from it. The freshness of your heart captivates Me; that is why I united Myself with you more closely than with any other creature[!]" (Diary, par. 1546)

- Etc.

» **rather weak / a pushover, who bends to her desires and whose hands can be "tied" - for example, consider these passages...**

- "On one occasion the Lord said to me, My daughter, your confidence and love restrain My justice, and I cannot inflict punishment because you hinder Me from doing so." (Diary, par. 198)

- "After Holy Communion, Jesus said to me, I cannot suffer that country any longer. Do not tie my hands, My daughter." (Diary, par. 818) *[She is more powerful than Jesus?]*

- "I heard these words: If you did not tie My hands, I would send down many punishments upon the earth. My daughter, your look disarms My anger. Although your lips are silent, you call out to Me so mightily that all heaven is moved. I cannot escape from your requests, because you pursue Me, not from afar but within your own heart." (Diary, par. 1722)

- "I have heard these words: My daughter, delight of My heart, it is with pleasure that I look into your soul. I bestow many graces only because of you. I also withhold My punishments only because of you. You restrain Me, and I cannot vindicate the claims of My justice. You bind My hands with your love." (Diary, par. 1193)

- "Then I heard a voice in my soul: My dear daughter, I comply with your request." (Diary, par. 961)

- "I often pray for Poland, but I see that God is very angry with it because of its ingratitude. I exert all the strength of my soul to defend it. I constantly remind God of the promises of His mercy. When I see His anger, I throw myself trustingly into the abyss of His mercy, and I plunge all Poland in it, and then He cannot use His justice. My country, how much you cost me! There is no day in which I do not pray for you." (Diary, par. 1188)

- "Be grateful for the smallest of My graces, because your gratitude compels Me to grant you new graces" (Diary, par. 1701)

- "Your great trust in Me forces Me to continuously grant you graces." (Diary, par. 718) *[Forced to - as if against His will?]*

- "I cannot punish even the greatest sinner if he makes an appeal to My compassion" (Diary, par. 1146)

» **preferential / picks favorites - for example, consider these passages...**

- "That is why I am uniting Myself with you so intimately as with no other creature." (Diary, par. 707)

- "At that moment, I prayed to the Lord for a certain person, and the Lord answered me, This soul is particularly dear to Me." (Diary, par. 1671)

- "And Jesus answered, And as for Me, I bestow special graces on those souls for whom you intercede." (Diary, par. 599)

- "Those whom you love in a special way, I too love in a special way, and for your sake, I shower My graces upon them." (Diary, par. 739)

- "My beloved native land, Poland, if you only knew how many sacrifices and prayers I offer to God for you! But be watchful and give glory to God, who lifts you up and singles you out in a special way." (Diary, par. 1038)

- "As I was praying for Poland, I heard the words: I bear a special love for Poland" (Diary, par. 1732) *[Yet she also writes: "I often pray for Poland, but I see that God is very angry with it because of its ingratitude." (Diary, par. 1188) So God is very angry with Poland, but simultaneously Poland is also extra special to Him?]*

- "When I had gone to the chapel for a moment, the Lord gave me to know that, among His chosen ones, there are some who are especially chosen[!], and whom He calls to a higher form of holiness, to exceptional union with Him." (Diary, par. 1556)

- "Jesus gave me to know how much this pleased Him, and my soul was filled with even greater joy to see that God loves in a special way those whom we love." (Diary, par. 1438)

- She also has Jesus' Blessed Mother saying, "I am the Queen of heaven and earth, but especially the Mother of your [Congregation]. She pressed me to Her heart and said, I feel constant compassion for you." (Diary, par. 805)

- "I hurry to their aid, shielding them with My Mercy, and I give them the first place in My compassionate Heart." (Diary, par. 1682)

- "I felt entirely like a child of God, and the Lord said to me, Fear nothing. What has been forbidden to others has been given to you. The graces that are not given to other souls to discern, not even from a distance, nourish you every day, like the daily bread." (Diary, par. 1753)

- "I know that I am under Your special gaze, O Lord." (Diary, par. 761)

» sensitive - for example, consider these passages...

- "I saw the Lord, who clasped to me to His Heart and said to me, My daughter, do not weep, for I cannot bear your tears. I gill grant you everything you ask for, but stop crying." (Diary, par. 928)

- "At that moment, I saw the Lord Jesus, His eyes filled with tears, and He said to me, You see, My daughter, what great compassion I have for them. Know that it is they who uphold the world." (Diary, par. 286)

- "Oh, how painful it is to Me that souls so seldom unite themselves to Me in Holy Communion." (Diary, par. 1447)

- "Know that you grieve Me much when you fail to receive Me in Holy Communion." (Diary, par. 156)

- "Oh, how much I am hurt by a soul's distrust!" (Diary, par. 300)

- "After a while a brightness filled my cell, and on the curtain I saw the very sorrowful Face of Jesus. There were open wounds on His Face, and large tears were falling on my bedspread. Not knowing what all this meant, I asked Jesus, 'Jesus, who has hurt You so?' And Jesus said to me, It is you who will cause Me this pain if you leave this convent. It is to this place that I called you and nowhere else; and I have prepared many graces for you. I begged pardon of Jesus and immediately changed my decision." (Diary, par. 19)

- "But souls do not even pay any attention to Me; they leave Me to Myself and busy themselves with other things. Oh, how sad I am that souls do not recognize Love! They treat Me as a dead object." (Diary, par. 1385)

- "I saw the Lord Jesus who said to me, Know, My daughter, that you caused Me more sorrow by not uniting yourself with Me in Holy Communion than you did by that small transgression." (Diary, par. 612)

- "How painfully distrust of My goodness wounds Me!" (Diary, par. 1076)

- "Today I learned with what aversion the Lord comes to a certain soul in Holy Communion. He goes to that heart as to a dark prison, to undergo torture and affliction." (Diary, par. 1280)

- "The loss of each soul plunges Me into mortal sadness." (Diary, par. 1397)

- "At ten, I saw the Sorrowful Face of Jesus. Then Jesus spoke these words to me: I have been waiting to share My suffering with you, for who can understand My suffering better than My spouse?" (Diary, par. 348) *[He didn't even speak this way with the Apostles or His blessed Mother, did He?]*

- "So I turn to you, you – chosen souls, will you also fail to understand the love of My Heart? Here, too, My Heart finds disappointment; I do not find complete surrender to My love. So many reservations, so much distrust, so much caution. ... The infidelity of a soul especially chosen by Me wounds My Heart most painfully. Such infidelities are swords which pierce My Heart." (Diary, par. 367)

- Etc.

» constantly reassuring / consoling / comforting / cheering her on - for example, consider these passages...

- "I suddenly saw Jesus, who looked at me penetratingly and said with ineffable sweetness, Your prayer is extremely pleasing to Me." (Diary, par. 691)

- "I saw Jesus in a brightness greater than the light of the sun. Jesus looked at me with love and said, Heart of My Heart, be filled with joy" (Diary, par. 1669)

- "In the evening, the Lord said to me, My child, rest on My Heart; I see that you have worked hard in my vineyard. And my soul was flooded with divine joy." (Diary, par. 945)

- "Jesus said to me, Be at peace; I am with you." (Diary, par. 1676)

- "I heard a voice in my soul: These efforts of yours, My daughter, are pleasing to Me; they are the delight of My Heart." (Diary, par. 1176)

- "I saw the Lord Jesus radiant as the sun, in a bright garment, and He said to me, May your heart be joyful." (Diary, par. 415)

- "When I came out of the house, I looked at the garden and the house, and when I cast a glance at the novitiate, tears suddenly ran down my cheeks. I remembered all the blessings and graces bestowed on me by the Lord. Then, suddenly and unexpectedly, I saw the Lord by the flower bed and He said to me, Do not weep; I am with you always." (Diary, par. 259)

- "During prayer, I heard these words: My daughter, let your heart be filled with joy. I, the Lord, am with you. Fear nothing. You are in My heart." (Diary, par. 1133)

- "Then the Lord looked at me kindly and comforted me with these words: Do not cry..." (Diary, par. 1703)

- Etc.

» **sad - for example, consider these passages...**

- "Why are You sad today, Jesus? Tell me, who is the cause of Your sadness? And Jesus answered me. Chosen souls who do not have my spirit, who live according to the letter [cf. 2 Cor. 3:6] and have placed the letter above My spirit, above the spirit of love. I have founded My whole law on love, and yet I do not see love, even in religious orders. This is why sadness fills My Heart." (Diary, par. 1478)

- "But souls do not even pay any attention to Me; they leave Me to Myself and busy themselves with other things. Oh, how sad I am that souls do not recognize Love! They treat Me as a dead object." (Diary, par. 1385)

- "I am sad when souls ask for little" (Diary, par. 1578)

» **complaining - for example, consider these passages...**

- "This distrust of My goodness hurts Me very much." (Diary, par. 580)

- "You know what a burden their souls are to My Heart." (Diary, par. 975)

- "During Holy Hour today, Jesus complained to me about the ingratitude of souls: In return for My blessings, I get ingratitude. In return for My love, I get forgetfulness and indifference. My Heart cannot bear this." (Diary, par. 1537)

- "Jesus complained to me in these words, Distrust on the part of souls is tearing at My insides." (Diary, par. 50)

» still suffering - for example, consider these passages...

- "Often a soul wounds Me mortally, and then no one can comfort Me." (Diary, par. 580)

- "I saw how unwillingly the Lord Jesus came to certain souls in Holy Communion. And He spoke these words to me: I enter into certain hearts as into a second Passion." (Diary, par. 1598)

- "The flames of compassion burn Me." (Diary, par. 1190)

- "The flames of mercy are burning me. I desire to pour them out upon human souls. Oh, what pain they cause Me when they do not want to accept them!" (Diary, par. 1074)

- Etc.

» desperate sounding - for example, consider these passages...

- "The loss of these souls plunges Me into deadly sorrow." (Diary, par. 580)

- "Distrust on the part of souls is tearing at My insides." (Diary, par. 50)

- "I want to give Myself to souls; I yearn for souls" (Diary, par. 206)

- "The flames of mercy are burning Me – clamoring to be spent" (Diary, par. 50)

- "My daughter, I want to repose in your heart, because many souls have thrown Me out of their hearts today. I have experienced sorrow unto death." (Diary, par. 866)

» in need of help - for example, consider these passages...

- "You know what a burden their souls are to My Heart. Relieve My deathly sorrow; dispense My mercy." (Diary, par. 975)

- "Today, the Lord came to me and said, My daughter, help Me to save souls." (Diary, par. 1797)

- "My daughter, help Me to save a certain dying sinner." (Diary, par. 1565)

- "Today, I saw the suffering Lord Jesus. He leaned down toward me and whispered softly, My daughter, help Me to save sinners." (Diary, par. 1645)

- "Today the Lord said to me, I have need of your sufferings to rescue souls." (Diary, par. 1612)

- "After some time, He said, I thirst. I thirst for salvation of souls. Help Me, My daughter, to save souls." (Diary, par. 1032)

» ostensibly lacking some knowledge (he asks questions, he is 'looking for souls' to lavish graces on) - for example, consider these passages...

- "Suddenly Jesus stood before me and said, What are you doing here so early? I answered, 'I am thinking of You, of Your mercy and Your goodness toward us. And You, Jesus what are You doing here?' I have come out to meet you, to lavish new graces on you. I am looking for souls who would like to receive My grace." (Diary, par. 1705) *[He is "looking for" souls - he doesn't have all knowledge?]*

- "Today, the Lord said to me, My daughter, I am told that there is much simplicity in you, so why do you not tell Me about everything that concerns you, even the smallest details?" (Diary, par. 921) *[He 'is told' of her simplicity? He has to be told something by others?]*

- "Now I know that it is not for the graces or gifts that you love me, but because My will is dearer to you than life" (Diary, par. 707) *[He didn't know before?]*

- "Then I heard the words: My daughter, have you exhausted the subject I gave you?" (Diary, par. 1756)

- "Jesus said to me, My daughter, have you any difficulties in this retreat?" (Diary, par. 1772)

- "I saw the Lord Jesus leaning over me, and He asked, My daughter, what are you writing?" (Diary, par. 1693)

- "Jesus stood by my side and said. My daughter, what are you thinking about right now?" (Diary, par. 960)

- "This evening, Jesus said to me, My daughter, do you need anything?" (Diary, par. 1682)

- "This evening, the Lord asked me, Do you not have any desires in your heart?" (Diary, par. 1700)

» **capable of being "surprised" and "very surprised" - for example, consider these passages...**

- "I am surprised that you still have not completely renounced your self-will." (Diary, par. 369) *[The all-knowing God is surprised?]*

- "Yes, when you are obedient I take away your weakness and replace it with My strength. I am very surprised [!] that souls do not want to make that exchange with Me." (Diary, par. 381)

» **reluctant to exercise justice - for example, consider these passages...**

- "My hand is reluctant to take hold of the sword of justice." (Diary, par. 1588)

- "[I head an interior voice] which said, My mercy does not want this [referring to Purgatory], but justice demands it. Since that time, I am in closer communion with the suffering souls." (Diary, par. 20)

- "Out of love for you all, I will avert any punishments which are rightly meted out by My Father's justice" (Diary, par. 570)

» **talkative during Mass (even as an infant) - for example, consider these passages...**

- "During Mass today, I saw the Lord Jesus, who said to me, Be at peace, My daughter; I see your efforts, which are very pleasing to Me. And the Lord disappeared, and it was time for Holy Communion." (Diary, par. 757)

- "Today, during the religious ceremonies taking place during Mass, and the second day of thanksgiving, I saw the Lord Jesus in great beauty, and He said to me..." (Diary, par. 1374)

- "Today, during Mass, I saw the Lord Jesus in the midst of His sufferings, as though dying on the cross. He said to me..." (Diary, par. 1512)

- "During Holy Mass, offered by Father Andrasz, I saw the little Infant Jesus, who told me that I was to depend on him for everything..." (Diary, par. 659)

- "During Holy Mass, which was celebrated by Father Andrasz, I saw the Infant Jesus who, with hands outstretched toward us, was sitting in the chalice [!] being used at Holy Mass. After gazing at me penetratingly, He spoke these words..." (Diary, par. 1346)

- "I was present at Holy Mass celebrated by Father Sopocko. During the Mass, I saw the Infant Jesus who, touching the priest's forehead with His finger, said to me, His thought is closely united to Mine, so be at peace about what concerns My work..." (Diary, par. 1408)

- Etc.

» **repetitive - for example, consider these passages...**

- "Jesus made the sign of the cross and said, Do not fear anything; I am always with you." (Diary, par. 613)

- "Then he spoke these words to me, My daughter, have fear of nothing; I am always with you." (Diary, par. 431)

- "I heard these words: Do not be afraid; I am always with you." (Diary, par. 627)

- "I heard these words: Do not fear anything. I am always with you." (Diary, par. 629)

- "Then he said to me, My daughter, fear nothing. I am always with you..." (Diary, par. 1109)

- "I heard these words: My daughter, I am always with you..." (Diary, par. 1267)

- "I heard a voice in my soul: Do not fear, My little child, you are not alone." (Diary, par. 1452)

- "Jesus looked at me kindly and said, My daughter, do not be afraid of sufferings; I am with you." (Diary, par. 151)

- Etc.

» **an 'Indian giver' - for example, consider this passage...**

"Write for the benefit of religious souls that it delights Me to come to their hearts in Holy Communion. But if there is anyone else in such a heart, I cannot bear it and quickly leave that heart, taking with Me all the gifts and graces I have prepared for the soul." (Diary, par. 1683)

» **and one who gives instant feedback - for example, consider these passages...**

- "When I complained to the Lord that He was taking my help away and that I would be alone again and would not know what to do, I heard these words: Do not be afraid; I am always with you. After these words, a deep peace once again entered my soul. His presence penetrated me completely in a way that could be sensed. My spirit was flooded with light, and my body participated in this as well." (Diary, par. 627)

- "When I entered the chapel for a five-minute adoration, I asked the Lord Jesus how I should conduct myself during this retreat. Then I heard this voice in my soul: I desire that you be entirely transformed into love and that you burn ardently as a pure victim of love..." (Diary, par. 726)

- "Today I felt bad that a week had gone by and no one had come to visit me. When I complained to the Lord, He answered, Isn't it enough for you that I visit you every day? I apologized to the Lord and the hurt vanished. O God, my strength, You are sufficient for me." (Diary, par. 827)

- "Jesus told me that if I should have any doubts regarding the feast or the founding of the Congregation - or regarding anything else about which I have spoken in the depths of your soul, I will reply immediately through the mouth of this priest." (Diary, par. 463)

- "During adoration, I felt so strongly urged to act that I burst into tears and said to the Lord, 'Jesus, do not urge me, but give this inspiration to those who You know are delaying the work.' And I heard these words: My daughter, be at peace; it will not be long now." (Diary, par. 865)

- "Once my confessor [Father Sopocko] asked me where the inscription should be placed, because there was not enough space in the picture for everything. In answered, 'I will pray and give you an answer next week.' When I left the confessional and was passing before the Blessed Sacrament, I received an inner understanding about the inscription." (Diary, par. 327)

- "As I usually do, I asked the Lord Jesus one evening to give me the points for next day's meditation. I received the answer: Meditate on the Prophet Jonah..." (Diary, par. 331)

- "Today, I received some oranges. When the sister had left, I thought to myself, 'Should I eat the oranges instead of doing penance and mortifying myself during Holy Lent? After all, I am feeling a bit better.' Then I heard a voice in my soul: My daughter, you please Me more by eating the oranges out of obedience and love of Me than by fasting and mortifying yourself of your own will..." (Diary, par. 1023)

- Etc.

» tries to delay suffering - for example, consider this passage...

"I received Holy Communion upstairs, for there was no question of my going down to the chapel since I was exhausted because of intense sweating, and when that passed, I had a fever and chills. I felt completely worn out. Today, one of the Jesuit Fathers [Father Zukowicz] brought us Holy Communion. He gave the Lord to three other sisters and then to me; and thinking I was the last, he gave me two Hosts. But one of the novices was lying in bed in the next cell, and there was no Host left for her. The priest went back again and brought her the Lord, but Jesus told me, I enter that heart unwillingly.

You received those two Hosts, because I delayed My coming into this soul who resists My grace. My visit to such a soul is not pleasant for Me." (Diary, par. 1658) *[Seriously? This is supposed to be the same Jesus who willingly endured the agonizing Passion?]*

» **'demands' a lot [her diary speaks of God 'demanding' various things from her, yet I do not see in Scripture where Jesus ever told anyone personally that he 'demanded' something in particular from them] - for example, consider these passages...**

- "Once during an adoration, the Lord demanded that I give myself up to Him as an offering" (Diary, par. 190)

- "God demands that there be a congregation which will proclaim the mercy of God to the world..." (Diary, par. 436)

- "I demand the worship of My mercy through the solemn celebration of the Feast and through the veneration of the image which is painted." (Diary, par. 742)

- "Jesus demanded that I should write more" (Diary, par. 1457)

- "Once, exhausted because of these various difficulties that had befallen me because of what Jesus had said to me and what He had demanded of me for the painting of this image..." (Diary, par. 52)

- "I demand of you a childlike spirit." (Diary, par. 332)

- "Oh, how ardently I desire to see this Feast of the Divine Mercy which God is demanding through me" (Diary, par. 711)

- "My daughter, if I demand through you that people revere My mercy, you should be the first to distinguish yourself by this confidence in My mercy. I demand from you deeds of mercy, which are to arise out of love for Me." (Diary, par. 742)

- "O most sweet Jesus, who have graciously demanded that I tell the whole world of Your incomprehensible mercy..." (Diary, par. 836)

- "My daughter, I demand that you devote all your free moments to writing about My goodness and mercy." (Diary, par. 1567) *[God demands that Faustina write about Him in her own personal diary, yet we never hear the Evangelists say God 'demanded' that they write Holy Scripture - which is obviously immeasurably, incomparably more important than Faustina's personal writings]*

- Etc.

» **discloses new doctrine (see above)**

» **speaks uncharacteristically (see above)**

» **lavishes praise on Faustina (see above)**

» **tasks her with instructing priests & superiors (see above)**

» **and is someone who would make odd requests, impersonate a priest, and who would seem to prefer Faustina's company rather than being in heaven - for example, consider these passages...**

- "Go to Mother Superior and tell her that you came back, not in order to reach home before dark, but because I had taken your heart" (Diary, par. 42)

- "Jesus listened to my words with gravity and kindness and spoke these words to me: Tell your confessor that I commune with your soul in such an intimate manner because you do not steal My gifts, and this is why I pour all these graces upon your soul, because I know that you will not hoard them for yourself." (Diary, par. 1069)

- "I heard these words: Tell the Superior General to count on you as the most faithful daughter in the Order." (Diary, par. 1130)

- "When I reflected that I had not been to confession for more than three weeks, I wept seeing the sinfulness of my soul and certain difficulties. I had not gone to confession because the circumstances made it impossible. On the day of confessions, I had been confined to bed. The following week, confessions were in the afternoon, and I had left for the hospital that morning. This afternoon, Father Andrasz came into my room and sat down to hear my confession. Beforehand, we did not exchange a single word. I was delighted because I was extremely anxious to go to confession. As usual, I unveiled my whole soul. Father gave a reply to each little detail. I felt unusually happy to be able to say everything as I did. For penance, he gave me the Litany of the Holy Name of Jesus. When I wanted to tell him of the difficulty I have in saying this litany, he rose and began to give me absolution. Suddenly his figure became diffused with a great light, and I saw that it was not Father A., but Jesus. His garments were bright as snow, and He disappeared immediately." (Diary, par. 817)

- "During Holy Mass I saw Jesus, and He said to me, You are My great joy; your love and your humility make Me leave the heavenly throne and unite Myself with you." (Diary, par. 512)

» **and who blesses her pen, moves a cloud to increase her comfort, instructs her in interpersonal communication, advises her regarding eating, arranges a retreat for her, has a private room prepared for her, helps her with her chores, offers her a new world to live in, promises her a permanent income...**

- **Blesses pen**: "As I took the pen in hand, I addressed a short prayer to the Holy Spirit and said, 'Jesus, bless this pen so that everything You order me to write may be for the glory of God.' Then I heard a voice: Yes, I bless [it], because this writing bears the seal of obedience to your superior and confessor, and by that very fact I am already given glory, and many souls will be drawing profit from it." (Diary, par. 1567)

- **Moves cloud to increase her comfort**: "It was so very hot that, even without working, a person felt terrible, not to mention what it was like when one had to work while suffering. So, before noon, I straightened up from my work, looked up to the sky with great trust and said to the Lord, 'Jesus, cover the sun, for I cannot stand this heat any longer.' And, O wonder, at that very moment a white cloud covered the sun and, from then on, the heat became less intense." (Diary, par. 701) *[All the other terrible sufferings Faustina writes about and she couldn't bear the heat?]*

- **Interpersonal communication advice**: "Before Holy Communion, Jesus gave me to understand that I should pay absolutely no attention to what a certain sister would say, because her cunning and malice were displeasing to Him. My daughter, do not speak to this person about either your views or your opinions. I begged the Lord's pardon for what in that soul was displeasing to Him, and I begged Him to strengthen me with His grace when she would come to talk with me again. She has asked me about many things, to which I gave answer with all my sisterly love and, as evidence that I have spoken to her from the bottom of my heart, I have told her some things that came from my own experience. But her intentions were something quite different from the words on her lips..." (Diary, par. 1492)

- **Advice regarding eating**: "Today, I received some oranges. When the sister had left, I thought to myself, 'Should I eat the oranges instead of doing penance and mortifying myself during Holy Lent? After all, I am feeling a bit better.' Then I heard a voice in my soul: My daughter, you please Me more by eating the oranges out of obedience and love of Me than by fasting and mortifying yourself of your own will..." (Diary, par. 1023)

- **Arranges retreat for her**: "After dinner, I went into the chapel for a five-minute adoration. Suddenly I saw the Lord Jesus, who said to me, My daughter, I am preparing many graces for you, which you will receive during this retreat which you will begin tomorrow. I answered, 'Jesus, the retreat has already begun, and I am not supposed to go.' And He said to me, Get ready for it, because you will begin the retreat tomorrow. And as for your departure, I will arrange that with the superiors. And in an instant, Jesus disappeared." (Diary, par. 167)

- **Has private room prepared for her**: "I was very worried that I would be put in bed in a ward and be exposed to all sorts of things. If it were to be for only a week or two... But it is for such a long time, two months or perhaps more. In the evening, I went in for a long talk with the Lord Jesus. When I saw the Lord Jesus, I poured out my whole heart before Him, all my troubles, fears and apprehensions. Jesus lovingly listened to me and then said, Be at peace, My child, I am with you. Go in great peace. All is ready; I have ordered, in My own special way, a private room to be prepared for you. Reassured and overwhelmed with gratitude, I went to bed." (Diary, par. 1674)

- **Helps her with chores**: "One time during the novitiate, when Mother Directress sent me to work in the wards' kitchen, I was very upset because I could not manage the pots, which were very large. The most difficult task for me was draining the potatoes, and sometimes, I spilt half of them with the water. When I told this to Mother Directress, she said that with time I would get used to it and gain the necessary skill. Yet the task was not getting any easier, as I was growing weaker every day. So I would move away when it was time to drain the potatoes. The sisters noticed that I avoided this task and were very much surprised. They did not know that I could not help in spite of all my willingness to do this and not spare myself. At noon, during the examination of conscience, I complained to God about my weakness. Then I heard the following words in my soul. From today on you will do this easily; I shall strengthen you. That evening, when the time came to drain off the water from the potatoes, I hurried to be the first to do it, trusting in the Lord's words. I took up the pot with ease and poured off the water perfectly. But when I took off the cover to let the potatoes steam off, I saw there in the pot, in the place of the potatoes, whole bunches of red roses, beautiful beyond description. I had never seen such roses before. Greatly astonished and unable to understand the meaning of this, I heard a voice within me saying, I change such hard work of yours into bouquets of most beautiful flowers, and their perfume rises up to My throne. From then on I have tried to drain the potatoes myself, not only during my week when it was my turn to cook, but also in replacement of other sisters when it was their turn. And not only do I do this, but I try to be the first to help in any other burdensome task, because I have experienced how much this pleases God." (Diary, par. 65) *[Note that she doesn't write that anyone else actually saw the flowers in the pot]*

- **Offers her a new world to live in**: "Once, I suddenly saw Jesus in great majesty, and He spoke these words to me: My daughter, if you wish, I will this instant create a new world, more beautiful than this one, and you will live there for the rest of your life." (Diary, par. 587)

- **Promises her a permanent income**: "Suddenly I head these words in my soul: My daughter, I assure you of a permanent income on which you will live." (Diary, par. 548)

#C - FAUSTINA SEEMS...

Faustina herself seems...

» **overly dramatic**

- "I must do violence to myself in order to live." (Diary, par. 899)

- "My soul is in a sea of suffering." (Diary, par. 893)

- "I cannot keep this happiness locked in my own heart alone, for His flames burn Me and cause my bosom and my entrails to burst asunder." (Diary, par. 491)

- "The greatness of God is pervading my being and flooding me so that I am completely drowning in His greatness." (Diary, par. 983)

- "Misery is my possession" (Diary, par. 1630)

- "I feel so terribly unwell in the morning; I have to muster all my strength to get out of bed, sometimes even to the point of heroism." (Diary, par. 1310)

- "my soul dissolved from the pain" (Diary, par. 1060)

- "When I meditate on this, my spirit swoons, and my heart dissolves in joy." (Diary, par. 1553)

- "if this continues a moment longer my heart will burst with grief" (Diary, par. 1562)

- "I have willingly allowed myself to be crucified, and I am indeed already crucified; although I can still walk a little" (Diary, par. 1580)

- "such an extraordinary disgust with life came over me that I had to make a great act of the will to consent to go on living" (Diary, par. 1497)

- "Once, I desired very much to receive Holy Communion, but I had a certain doubt, and I did not go. I suffered greatly because of this. It seemed to me that my heart would burst from the pain" (Diary, par. 156)

- "And at that moment, such terrible torment overwhelmed me that now I am amazed at myself that I did not breathe my last, but this was for only a brief instant." (Diary, par. 1558)

- "my heart was burning with a love so strong that it seemed my breast would burst" (Diary, par. 1705)

- "No one can understand or comprehend, nor can I myself describe, my torments. But there can be no sufferings greater than this. The sufferings of the martyrs are not greater because, at such times, death would be a relief for me. There is nothing to which I can compare these sufferings, this endless agony of the soul." (Diary, par. 1116)

- "my heart dissolved in love and bitterness." (Diary, par. 1054)

- "Today, I came to know that a member of my family is offending God and is in great peril of death. This knowledge pierced my soul with such great pain that I thought I would not survive that offense against God." (Diary, par. 987)

- Etc.

» pretty sensitive

- "When I hear the sweetest name of Jesus, my heartbeat grows stronger, and there are times when, hearing the Name of Jesus, I fall into a swoon." (Diary, par. 862)

- "Today, I came to know that a member of my family is offending God and is in great peril of death. This knowledge pierced my soul with such great pain that I thought I would not survive that offense against God." (Diary, par. 987)

- "Once, I desired very much to receive Holy Communion, but I had a certain doubt, and I did not go. I suffered greatly because of this. It seemed to me that my heart would burst from the pain" (Diary, par. 156)

- "During both hours I saw the Lord Jesus as he was after the scourging. My soul felt such great pain that it seemed to me that I was experiencing all those torments in my own body and in my own soul." (Diary, par. 614)

- "My spirit is so pervaded with God that I feel it physically" (Diary, par. 582)

- "I could clearly feel how the hymns of Hosanna reverberated as a painful echo in His Sacred Heart. My soul, too, was inundated by a sea of bitterness, and each Hosanna pierced my own heart to its depths." (Diary, par. 1657)

- Etc.

» emotional

- "I burst into tears of joy like a little child" (Diary, par. 1551)

- "During adoration, I felt so strongly urged to act that I burst into tears" (Diary, par. 865)

- "and I wept like a child that there was no saint in our midst. And I said to the Lord, 'I know Your generosity, and yet it seems to me that You are less generous toward us.' And I began again to weep like a little child." (Diary, par. 1650)

- "In the evening, over the radio, I heard hymns; that is, psalms, sung by priests. I burst into tears, and all of the pain was renewed in my soul, and I wept sorrowfully, unable to find appeasement in this pain." (Diary, par. 1061)

- "When I came out of the house, I looked at the garden and the house, and when I cast a glance at the novitiate, tears suddenly ran down my cheeks. I remembered all the blessings and graces bestowed on me by the Lord. Then, suddenly and unexpectedly, I saw the Lord by the flower bed and He said to me, Do not weep; I am with you always." (Diary, par. 259)

- Etc.

» insensitive to other's concerns with respect to herself (she seems unable to see things from their perspective)

Nowhere do I see where she understands that her odd claims might reasonably be questioned by others. Rather, her diary contains passages like these...

> "All these things could still be endured. But when the Lord demanded that I should paint that picture, they began to speak openly about me and to regard me as a hysteric and a fantasist, and the rumors began to grow louder. One of the sisters came to talk to me in private. She began by pitying me and said, 'I've heard them say that you are a fantasist, Sister, and that you've been having visions. My poor Sister, defend yourself in this matter.' She was a sincere soul, and she told me sincerely what she had heard. But I had to listen to such things every day. God only knows how tiring it was." (Diary, par. 125) *[Note how she seems to have no understanding of why others would reasonably think as they do.]*

"A certain sister is constantly persecuting me for the sole reason that God communes with me so intimately, and she thinks that this is all pretense on my part. When she thinks that I have done something amiss she says, 'Some people have revelations, but commit such faults!' She has said this to all the sisters and always in a derogatory sense, in order to make me out as some sort of an oddity. One day, it caused me much pain to think that this insignificant drop which is the human brain can so easily scrutinize the gifts of God. After Holy Communion, I prayed that the Lord would enlighten her, but nevertheless I learned that this soul will not attain perfection if she does not change her interior dispositions." (Diary, par. 1527) *[Again, Faustina indicates no understanding of why people might reasonably think as they do.]*

» rather easily annoyed

- "I have at present a little room in which two of us sleep, but at the time of my sickness when I had to stay in bed, I found out how bothersome it was if someone was sitting in the bedroom all the time. Sister N. had some handwork to do and sat in the bedroom almost all of the time, and another S. would come to instruct her on how to do it. It's difficult to describe how much this tires one, especially when one is ill and has spent a night in pain. Every word has a repercussion somewhere in the brain, especially when the eyes are heavy with sleep. O rule, how much love there is in you..." (Diary, par. 1476)

- "Toward the end of a three-day retreat, I saw myself walking along a rough path. I kept stumbling continually, and I saw following me the figure of a person who kept supporting me. I was not happy with this and asked the person to leave me alone, as I wanted to walk on my own. But the figure, whom I could not recognize, did not leave me for a moment. I got impatient and turned around and pushed the person away from me. At that moment I saw that it was Mother Superior [Irene], and at the same moment I saw that it was not Mother Superior, but the Lord Jesus who looked deeply into me and gave me to understand how painful it was to Him when I did not, even in the smallest things, do my Superior's will, which is My will, [He said]." (Diary, par. 329)

- Etc.

» **somewhat self-centered (e.g. about how people treat her, about what she suffers for others, about how people don't trust her alleged visions) (see above)**

» **up and down a lot ('an emotional roller coaster')**

- "At a certain point, there came to me the very powerful impression that I am rejected by God." (Diary, par. 23)

- "It seemed as though hell had conspired against me. A terrible hatred began to break out in my soul, a hatred for all that is holy and divine." (Diary, par. 25)

- "darkness continued to reign in my soul for almost a half year." (Diary, par. 27)

- "From the moment when You let me fix the eyes of my soul on You, O Jesus, I have been at peace and desired nothing else, I found my destiny at the moment when my soul lost itself in You, the only object of my love." (Diary, par. 57)

- "My mind became dimmed in a strange way; no truth seemed clear to me. When people spoke to me about God, my heart was like a rock. I could not draw from it a single sentiment of love for Him... I felt an aversion for the Holy Sacraments, and it seemed to me that I was not profiting from them in any way." (Diary, par. 77)

- "Once again, a terrible darkness envelops my soul. It seems to me that I am falling prey to illusions." (Diary, par. 211)

- "These words were so filled with power and so clear that I would give my life in declaring they came from God. I can tell this by the profound peace that accompanied them at that time and that still remains with me. This peace gives me such great strength and power that all difficulties, adversities, sufferings, and death itself are as nothing." (Diary, par. 359)

- "I cannot keep this happiness locked in my own heart alone, for His flames burn Me and cause my bosom and my entrails to burst asunder." (Diary, par. 491)

- "His divine gaze filled my heart with such joy that I have no words to express it." (Diary, par. 560)

- "At that moment, Jesus disappeared. My soul was filled with the presence of God. I know that the gaze of the Mighty One rests upon me. I plunged myself completely in the joy that flows from God. I continued throughout the whole day without interruption, thus immersed in God. In the evening, I fell as if into a faint and a strange sort of agony." (Diary, par. 708)

- "Today my soul is steeped in bitterness." (Diary, par. 896)

- "Today, I feel such desolation in my soul that I do not know how to explain it even to myself. I would like to hide from people and cry endlessly." (Diary, par. 943)

- "so my inner torture is so great that no one will either understand or imagine these spiritual sufferings. It seems to me that it would be easier to give up my life than to go again and again through one hour of such pain." (Diary, par. 981)

- "The Lord has poured such a depth of peace into my soul that nothing will disturb it any more. Despite everything that goes on around me, I am not deprived of my peace for a moment. Even if the whole world were crumbling, it would not disturb the depth of the silence which is within me and in which God rests. All events, all the various things which happen are under His foot." (Diary, par. 1134)

- "Today, my soul suffered such agony" (Diary, par. 1161)

- "Today, since early in the morning, my soul has been in darkness. I cannot ascend to Jesus, and I feel as though I have been forsaken by Him." (Diary, par. 1496)

- "Today is the Feast of the Mother of God, and in my soul it is so dark. The Lord has hidden Himself, and I am alone, all alone. My mind has become so dimmed that I see only phantasms about me. Not a single ray of light penetrates my soul. I do not understand myself or those who speak to me. Frightful temptations regarding the holy faith assail me. O my Jesus, save me. I cannot say anything more. I cannot describe these things in detail, for I fear lest someone be scandalized on reading this. I am astounded that such torments could befall a soul. O hurricane, what are you doing to the boat of my heart? This storm has lasted the whole day and night." (Diary, par. 1558)

- Etc.

» to need a lot of reassurance

- "See how weak I am! I cannot go a step forward by myself; so You, Jesus, must stand by me constantly like a mother by a helpless child – and even more so." (Diary, par. 264)

- "You know well how weak I am of myself; that is why I know that it is my weakness that forces [!] You to be with me constantly." (Diary, par. 569)

» sometimes lacking in fear of the Lord

- "the living Lord Jesus...said to me, I will stay here no longer! At this, a powerful love for Jesus rose up in my soul, I answered, 'And I, I will not let You [!] leave this house, Jesus!'" (Diary, par. 44)

- "I saw the Lord Jesus as He is represented in the image. Jesus was walking away, and I called to Him, 'How can You pass me by and not say anything to me, Lord? Without You, I shall do nothing; You must [!] stay with me and bless me, and this community and my country as well'" (Diary, par. 613)

- "Jesus stood by my side and said. My daughter, what are you thinking about right now? Without thinking, I snuggled close [!] to His heart" (Diary, par. 960)

- "I brought my head close to the tabernacle, knocked [!] and said, 'Jesus, look at the great difficulties I am having because of the painting of this image.'" (Diary, par. 152)

- Note what she calls Jesus: "At the feet of the Lord. Hidden Jesus, Eternal Love, our Source of Life, divine Madman[!], in that You forget yourself and see only us." (Diary, par. 278)

- Etc.

» **to lack normal reactions to having a life filled with alleged supernatural events/promises (humdrum, day to day - yet she claims to be united with God like no other person before and to have a special closeness, a more intimate relationship with Jesus than all others) (see above)**

» **naïve / credulous / not discerning**

For example...

- She burned her diary after she claims she was told to do so by a heavenly being (an angel, 'who turned out to be a devil'),

211

despite the fact that she emphasizes how she writes only out of obedience

- She made a dishonest confession (see above) because someone told her to

- She talks with the devil on multiple occasions (see par. 320, 418, 520, 1127, 1405) even though this is dangerous

- She asks a Seraph to hear her confession (see par. 1677)

- She seems sometimes to be guided by her feelings (e.g. see par. 835: "Today I was awakened suddenly at eleven o'clock at night and clearly felt the presence near me of some spirit who was asking me for prayer. Some force simply compelled me to pray. My vision is purely spiritual, by means of a sudden light that God grants me at that moment. I keep on praying until I feel peace in my soul, and not always for an equally long time; because sometimes it happens that with one 'Hail Mary' I am already at peace, and then I say the De Profundis and pray no longer. And sometimes it happens that I pray the entire chaplet and only then feel at peace.")

» **narcissistic (self-important in her alleged mission, talks about the good she does, reproaches a saint)**

For example...

- See above regarding her 'mission'

- See above regarding 'grandiose thoughts'

- See above regarding good deeds

Also...

- She reproaches a saint: "Feast of St. Ignatius. I prayed fervently to this Saint, reproaching him for looking on and not coming to my aid in such important matters as doing the will of God." (Diary, par. 448)

- She is "astonished" that Jesus can hide Himself from her ("I am astonished, Jesus, that You can hide Yourself from me for so long and that You can restrain the enormous love You have for me.", Diary, par. 1239)

- She tells Satan that she is going to tell the WHOLE Church about her experience with him ("And I said to the wretched soul [Satan under the assumed appearance of this soul] that I would tell the whole Church about this", Diary, par. 520) *[Who - other than maybe a pope - would say they were going to tell the "whole Church" about something? Especially a female who tells us about how she practices humility?]*

- Even in her dreams, Faustina is concerned about whether or not she will be canonized. ("On the fifth day of the novena, I dreamed of Saint Therese, but it was as if she were still living on earth. She hid from me the fact that she was a saint and began to comfort me, saying that I should not be worried about this matter, but should trust more in God. She said, 'I suffered greatly, too, but I did not quite believe her and said, 'It seems to me that you have not suffered at all.' But Saint Therese answered me in a convincing manner that she had suffered very much indeed and said to me, 'Sister, know that in three days the difficulty will come to a happy conclusion.' When I was not very willing to believe her, she revealed to me that she was a saint. At that moment, a great joy filled my soul, and I said to her, 'You are a saint?' 'Yes,' she answered, 'I am a saint. Trust that this matter will be resolved in three days.' And I said, 'Dear sweet Therese, tell me, shall I go to heaven?' And she answered, 'Yes, you will go to heaven, Sister.' 'And will I be a saint?' 'But, little Therese, shall I be a saint as you are, raised to the altar?' And she answered, 'Yes, you will be a saint just as I am, but you must trust in the Lord Jesus.' ... This was a dream. And as the proverb goes, dreams are phantoms; God is faith. Nevertheless, three days later the difficulty was solved very easily, just as she had said. And everything in this affair turned out exactly as she said it would. It was a dream, but it had its significance.", Diary, par. 150)

» **seems to live in another world where visions are constant/common and normal (even if their content is disturbing and uncharacteristic of the alleged participants - where the Almighty God and the Mother of God & others are always at her beck and call for whatever her need may be) and those who question the alleged appearances just don't understand the graces she's received or they're in league with the devil (see above)**

» **sometimes weepy, yet more powerful than heavenly beings - she was even able to make an angel, the executor of divine wrath 'helpless', and she was able to calm storms, etc.**

- "After these words, my love made great efforts to express to Him what He was to me, but I was at a loss for words and burst into tears in my helplessness." (Diary, par. 1775)

- "I wept like a child that there was no saint in our midst... And I began again to weep like a little child." (Diary, par. 1650)

- "I burst into tears" (Diary, par. 1061, 1551)

- "During adoration, I felt so strongly urged to act that I burst into tears" (Diary, par. 865)

- "I heard these words: If you did not tie My hands, I would send down many punishments upon the earth. My daughter, your look disarms My anger. Although your lips are silent, you call out to Me so mightily that all heaven is moved. I cannot escape from your requests, because you pursue Me, not from afar but within your own heart." (Diary, par. 1722)

- "After Holy Communion, Jesus said to me, I cannot suffer that country any longer. Do not tie my hands [!], My daughter." (Diary, par. 818)

- "In the evening, when I was in my cell, I saw an Angel, the executor of divine wrath. He was clothed in a dazzling robe, his face gloriously bright, a cloud beneath his feet. From the cloud, bolts of thunder and flashes of lightning were springing into his hands; and from his hand they were going forth, and only then were they striking the earth. When I saw this sign of divine wrath which was about to strike the earth, and in particular a certain place, which for good reasons I cannot name, I began to implore the Angel to hold off for a few moments, and the world would do penance. But my plea was a mere nothing in the face of the divine anger. Just then I saw the Most Holy Trinity. The greatness of Its majesty pierced me deeply, and I did not dare to repeat my entreaties. At that very moment I felt in my soul the power of Jesus' grace, which dwells in my soul. When I became conscious of this grace, I was instantly snatched up before the Throne of God. Oh, how great is our Lord and God and how incomprehensible His holiness! I will make no attempt to describe this greatness, because before long we shall all see Him as He is. I found myself pleading with God for the world with words heard interiorly. As I was praying in this manner, I saw the Angel's helplessness[!]: he could not carry out the just punishment which was rightly due for sins." (Diary, par. 474) *[What was the executor of divine wrath doing in Faustina's cell in the first place?]*

- "When a great storm was approaching, I began to say the chaplet. Suddenly I heard the voice of an angel: 'I cannot approach in this storm, because the light which comes from her mouth drives back both me and the storm.' Such was the angel's complaint to God." (Diary, par. 1791)

- "There was a terrible storm last night. I bowed my face low to the ground and started to say the Litany of the Saints.

Towards the end of the Litany, such drowsiness came over me that I could in no way finish the prayer. Then I got up and said to the Lord, 'Jesus, calm the storm, for Your child is unable to pray any longer, and I am heavy with sleep.' After these words, I threw the window wide open, not even securing it with hooks. Sister N. [probably sister Fabiola Pawluk] then said to me, 'Sister, what are you doing! The wind will surely tear the window loose!' I told her to sleep in peace, and at once the storm completely subsided. The next day, the sisters talked about the sudden calming of the storm, not knowing what this meant. I said nothing, but I merely thought within myself: Jesus and little Faustina know what it means..." (Diary, par. 1197)

» **sometimes out of touch with reality / strange sense of reality**

In Faustina's world...

- Images come to life

- Crucifixes come to life *[Note that Faustina takes this all in stride & never mentions that she found the inch tall living 'Jesus' on her chest to be freaky!]*

- Jesus & Mary come down from heaven to hug and comfort her

- God, Mary, and the saints are at her 'beck and call' for instruction, answers, advice, comfort, etc.

- She is the object of excessive praise & is singled out for special care by God, the Blessed Virgin Mary, St. Michael, etc.

- The Infant Jesus supposedly sits in the chalice and runs on the altar

- Dead people can hug

- Voices & visions are commonplace

- Etc.

She even thinks she is on a stage where everyone is watching her...

> "[The voice said to her,] Know that you are now on a great stage where all heaven and earth are watching you." (Diary, par. 1760)

» **to have visions of grandeur (see above)**

» **to mention her sufferings and mistreatment a lot (see above)**

* * *

PART 3

Also Try / Additional Resources...

Divine Mercy (Topic Page):
http://www.mycatholicsource.com/mcs/tp/topic_page-divine_mercy.htm

Catholic News / Current Issues:
http://www.mycatholicsource.com/mcs/catholic_news.htm

Second Vatican Council (Topic Page):
http://www.mycatholicsource.com/mcs/tp/topic_page-second_vatican_council.htm

Traditional Catholic (Topic Page):
http://www.mycatholicsource.com/mcs/tp/topic_page-traditional_catholic.htm

Jesus (Topic Page):
http://www.mycatholicsource.com/mcs/tp/topic_page-Jesus.htm

Blessed Virgin Mercy (Topic Page):
http://www.mycatholicsource.com/mcs/tp/topic_page-Blessed_Virgin_Mary.htm

Tough Love in the New Testament:
http://www.mycatholicsource.com/mcs/pcs/nt_tough_love.htm

User Article: "'Great' Popes: When a Pope Should Be & Should Not Be Called Great":

http://www.mycatholicsource.com/mcs/ua/user_article-when_a_pope_should_be_called_great.htm

Prayers & Devotions Section:
http://www.mycatholicsource.com/mcs/prayers_and_devotions.htm

Submit a Comment About this Article ('add post'):
http://www.mycatholicsource.com/mcs/udi/ai/catholic_life_add.asp

Read Comments Regarding this Article (if applicable):
http://www.mycatholicsource.com/mcs/udi/vi/catholic_life_view.asp

Read Other User-Submitted Articles:
http://www.mycatholicsource.com/mcs/ua/user_articles_index.htm

Submit Your Own Article:
http://www.mycatholicsource.com/mcs/fdb/article_submission.htm

More About User-Submitted Articles:
http://www.mycatholicsource.com/mcs/ua/user_articles.htm

Read User-Submitted Posts:
http://www.mycatholicsource.com/mcs/where_to_find_posts.htm

Submit Your Own Post:
http://www.mycatholicsource.com/mcs/where_to_find_posts.htm

Visit Here For Thousands of Quotations From Popes, Saints, Scripture, Etc. Categorized By Section:
http://www.mycatholicsource.com/mcs/qt/reflections_categorized.htm

Looking For a Great Catholic Home Page? Try the MCS Daily Digest™:
http://www.mycatholicsource.com/mcs/cg/mcs_daily_digest.asp

Reminder: We make no guarantees regarding any item herein. By using this material, including links herein, you indicate agreement to

all terms. For terms information, visit
http://www.mycatholicsource.com/mcs/terms_of_use.htm

Made in United States
North Haven, CT
09 April 2023

35232446R00136